Open When

Open
When

A Companion
for Life's
Twists and Turns

DR. JULIE SMITH

HarperOne
An Imprint of HarperCollins*Publishers*

Extract on p. 119 from *The Concise Forty-Eight Laws of Power* by Robert Greene, copyright © 1998, 2002, by Robert Greene and Joost Elggers. Reprinted by kind permission of Profile Books.

Originally published as *Open When* in Great Britain in 2024 by Michael Joseph.

FIRST HARPERONE HARDCOVER PUBLISHED 2024

Designed by Janet Evans-Scanlon
Tools image used throughout © AAVAA/stock.adobe.com

Library of Congress Cataloging-in-Publication Data has been applied for.

ISBN 978-0-06-335926-0

24 25 26 27 28 LBC 5 4 3 2 1

For Sienna, Luke, and Leon.
My wish is that you never need this book.
But I wrote it just in case.

Contents

Contents

Part 3: When it's hard to be with your feelings

Introduction:
A letter from
me to you

Get busy with life's purpose, toss aside empty hopes, get
active in your own rescue—if you care for yourself at all—
and do it while you can.

—Marcus Aurelius, *Meditations*, 3.14

Despite the words laid out in front of you, I have never been a
talker. Even as a child, I observed and absorbed, but rarely
approached anyone in times of need. For that, I did what many
quiet kids do: I turned to books. Looking back, I see my impulse
to read as a kind of searching. I was asking of the pages what I
was unable to ask of real people. I waded through book after
book. Sometimes I found what I needed. Sometimes I didn't.

With that in mind and my current profession as a clinical
psychologist, you would be forgiven for assuming that I want to
promote inward-focused self-reflection. That is not the case.
The inner world is like a sauna; there are benefits to being there,
as long as you don't stay for too long. Instead, I strongly urge
you, in challenging times, to connect with other humans in the
real world wherever possible. That is where most of the answers
are to our naturally fluctuating mental health in the face of life's

ups and downs. But I am also realistic enough to know that not everybody has a reliable and trustworthy person available to them at the most crucial of times. When you find yourself working things out alone and you struggle to be the voice for yourself that you need to hear, this book is for you.

The moment I realized that I needed to write this book was when I heard stories of how people were carrying around my first book, *Why Has Nobody Told Me This Before?*, so that they could refer to it in difficult moments. While these stories were often shared with me as a compliment, I couldn't help but think that it wasn't written for that purpose. It was the wrong book for the job. That book is filled with the concepts and skills that help people to work on their future mental health, often by looking back at past difficult moments. Not one of those pages contains the words I say to people as they sit in their most vulnerable moments, raw with emotion.

In the days before a hurricane, a hammer and nails are exactly the tools you need to arm you for what might lie ahead. But the moment that storm hits, the last thing you need to hear is how you could have been better prepared. In those moments, what we all need is someone to look us straight in the eye and bring the words we need to hear right now. Words that say "I'm here. Let's move forward together. I know a way through." You might say my previous book was the hammer and nails. This book is my hand reaching out to yours in the chaos of the storm, saying "Come this way and let's get to work."

In moments of pain or confusion, most of us struggle to be the voice that we need to hear, not because we are pathological in some way, but because we are all simply learning as we go. This is the book for us all, for our children as they fly the nest, for our friends who live out of reach, for our family when we can't find the right words, and for ourselves when we need to find a way through.

With my own experience as both a reader and a clinician, I know that in dark times, words can light the way, illuminating a new path you didn't know existed. As I wrote these letters to you, which you'll find at the beginning of each chapter, I wished at times that I could read your mind and know precisely what you are dealing with and the words you need the most. An impossible task, since I can't predict the details of the challenges you face. Instead, all I have are the gems I have discovered along my own path and a chance to lay them out on yours.

This book can serve only as a lighthouse. Unable to pull you from the water, but able to shine a light in this direction so that you can work out which way is up when confusion reigns. Use that as you will, but the work of navigating toward calmer waters is all yours.

In the trials that lie ahead, I have high expectations for you because I can be sure of two things. First, that you have potential beyond anything you could comprehend from your current standpoint. Second, no matter where you are starting from, the path to all things better is always through new effort and willingness to learn. It is true for all of us that we don't know what we don't know. Please trust me when I say that you have no idea how much better things could get for you until you're there.

Kindest,

Julie

1

When it's hard to be with other people

CHAPTER 1

When you compare yourself and come up short

There is nothing noble in being superior to your fellow man; true nobility is being superior to your former self.

—Attributed to Ernest Hemingway

A letter from me to you

If you compare yourself to someone else and come up short, that can leave you in one of two places. You either feel inspired, energized, and motivated to learn from what you have seen is possible, or you fall uncontrollably into a downward spiral. If your experience is the second one, then the problem is not you and all of your apparent inadequacies, it's your comparisons.

If you have some underlying self-destructive beliefs about whether you are fundamentally good enough, then you will not be choosing comparisons that help your progress. You will be choosing comparisons that confirm those core beliefs, however damaging they may be. You will sit in full view of your own weaknesses and gaze at someone else's best show of strength as if this were a level playing field. You will not see that person in a fuller, more real way that incorporates all the parts of their life that they don't put on display. Even if you get a peek at their imperfections, you are likely to ignore them. You will put this person on such a pedestal in your own mind that the only way to lift yourself up will be to pull them down, turning you into the kind of person you never wanted to become.

If the people you compare yourself to are friends or family, then it can become a destructive force on your relationship. Comparison thwarts connection because it suggests that their success is your failure and carves out a path toward resentment and bitterness between you. The more isolated you become from the people in your life, the more that feeds such comparison. But getting to know those people more deeply is a counterforce to the type of comparison that poisons the relationship. The more deeply you know someone, the less you will be inclined to make such superficial and false judgments. You can form a friendship in which you can recognize your common humanity and see yourself as a team that supports each other in your different endeavors. Then you can start to be happy for their personal victories and genuinely compassionate when they face setbacks. When you get to know an individual, you start to realize that they don't share the same intricacies of life as your own and therefore make a terrible model for comparison.

So many people will tell you that it's simple: just stop comparing yourself to others. But it doesn't take long for you to try that and fail, and to see that it really is not that simple. Your tendency to compare is a built-in tool that is as helpful as it is dangerous.

When used right, it can steer you in the right direction, inspire you, and push you beyond your limits. When used in the wrong way, the damage it can do is far-reaching and long-lasting.

Comparing and coming up short doesn't have to be a bad thing. It doesn't mean that we should never have compared ourselves at all. If that comparison leads to constructive forward motion and a bolstered belief that we can become more than what we are today, then it served us well. If it leads to envy, resentment, bitterness, and a loss of self-worth, then we are getting it all wrong, and both our efforts and our attention have been misplaced in a way that could cost us heavily. What we need is to know how to use comparison to our advantage and to spot when it's self-destructive.

Real-time tools

These tools go beyond the usual dismissal of comparison with a "just stop doing it" approach. The natural human urge to understand our place in the world by looking to others is as much a part of our nature as the intake of breath. Telling you to just stop comparing yourself will, at best, stoke the fire of positivity in your belly for a few minutes. That fire will be easily blown out the next time you open your favorite social media app. Within seconds of walking into a room of peers, you feel a sense of your social or professional status in that room. The act of comparison itself is not always a set of thoughts. Your brain is working faster than that to establish how you should approach the situation you find yourself in. At the same time, you don't have to be at the mercy of the downward spiral that social comparison inflicts on your mind. There are things you can do to spot the destructive ways we compare ourselves and to make a conscious effort to redirect toward comparisons that can genuinely serve you.

What makes comparison destructive

Social media

It's difficult to self-evaluate without some level of comparison because we don't live in isolation. We live in communities that have norms and expectations for everyone. Comparison helps us avoid the humiliation, rejection, and loss of social status that might happen if we unwittingly breached those expectations. It helps us navigate all our social interactions throughout life, determine whether we're contributing enough and whether we're acting in ways that will be acceptable, and establish whom we want to emulate and whom we don't. How you measure up in your community matters if you want to navigate successfully within it. So your ability to engage in social comparison is not always your enemy. It's an essential life skill that you wouldn't do so well without.

But while it helps to consider your own surroundings as a part of self-evaluation, when you consult social media, what you're looking at is not your real community. In fact, much of it is not real at all. It's a collection of carefully crafted, digitally altered images that a person or company wants you to see.

And within minutes of you indulging in some wildly unfair and deeply unhelpful upward comparisons, the algorithm has mapped exactly what will keep your attention and feeds you a never-ending stream of the content that will make you sick. Rather than any social comparisons that might help you live your life most effectively, you have the most corrosive, poisonous comparisons on repeat that leave you feeling dissatisfied with yourself as a person and with the life that you could be out there enjoying.

The psychological toxicity produced by this whole process is either turned inward on ourselves in the form of self-loathing and depression or gets reflected outward in the malicious sabo-taging of those other people we have come to feel so bitter and resentful toward.[1] You don't need to scroll for long before you find hordes of keyboard warriors spewing their rage at another human being, picking at imperfections like hyenas at a wounded animal, with the attempt to bring them down a peg or two and to steer the perception of the group away from one of admira-tion for this person who dared do so well.

The urges to take someone else down online happen more than people will admit, but if you notice it in yourself, or the degeneration of satisfaction in your own life, it's time to turn away from social media and spend more time in real life with real people and real connections.

Comparing with loved ones

Outside social media, if you notice you're comparing yourself to someone who means a lot to you, a friend or family member, don't let it go unchecked. The damage can stretch beyond your own well-being and poses a risk to the whole relationship.

Friendships or family connections that could have been a posi-tive force in your life can rupture irreparably if you start measuring yourself against them. You cannot be a team if you set up the game so that you can't all win at the same time. Even if their goals don't match your own, the jealousy and resentment that ignite when something threatens to diminish your own social status is hard to acknowledge but will destroy a relationship if left to fester.

As Alain de Botton put it, "There are few successes more unendurable than those of our close friends."[2] Before you know it, you go from viewing yourself as someone who would always be happy to see friends succeed to finding it excruciating to be around them. Whether you avoid them, start excluding them from a wider group, or isolate yourself, the outcomes are dismal for everyone. These are the dark places where careless and nonconstructive comparisons can lead us.

When you avoid that particular friend, what you are really doing is avoiding the feelings their success has brought up in you. That knowledge is so valuable to you only if you are willing to look at it and be honest with yourself about whether you are happy with the direction your own life is moving in. When you are brave enough to look at those emotional reactions with curiosity rather than trying to eliminate them by bringing the friend down or avoiding them altogether, then you have a path toward resolution and the possibility of feeling genuinely happy for your friends when things go well for them. If your sense of self-worth is dependent on feeling superior to your friends and family in some way, then take that as a sign, not to reject them, but to reevaluate your own life. If you have your own values clear in your mind and you are living in line with them, then superficial signs of apparent success or failure are less earth-shattering than they might otherwise be.

When a friend finds a path to move up in the world, or is knocked down fighting their own demons, and if that brings up in you some very uncomfortable feelings, which it will, do not act with impulse to push against them, but instead listen to the feelings and ask yourself with genuine curiosity what those teach you about yourself. Sometimes it will be just fleeting emotions that pass and allow you to come back to feeling satisfied with your life. At other times it could spark some positive changes. But for that to happen, the comparison usually needs to be constructive. Here are some ideas for how to make comparisons helpful to you.

How to make comparison constructive

Turn envy into inspiration

When we use comparison in the correct way, we can take advantage of its power to influence how we feel and behave. Let's say you're working to improve your skills in your favorite sport and you know that you have a specific weakness that holds you back. In this scenario, some upward comparison with a player who has managed to master that skill offers you a huge opportunity to learn from them and improve your own skills in the process. But for that to happen successfully, your comparison needs to get these three elements right:

1. Keep a clear focus on the specific skill you envy in their performance. Be laser-focused on specifics and do not be tempted to make a global comparison between your whole self and theirs. You don't want to be that person, but there's something in the way they do things that you want to take on board and benefit from in your own life.

2. Prime yourself with a growth mindset. This means keeping in mind that you have agency in your own life and can learn and improve at most things with effort. This mindset will lead to positive action toward your own goals, as opposed to a more fixed mindset that assumes your abilities are

fixed and some people are just lucky. That fixed mindset will likely lead to more destructive comparisons, bitterness, and fractured relationships

3. Your self-worth remains nonnegotiable at all times. It should never be on the line. This is absolutely essential. If your estimation of yourself as worthwhile is measured by others, this is the rogue ingredient that will turn everything sour. Turning envy into inspiration is no problem at all as long as you are not measuring your self-worth by how other people seem to be doing. We can all find someone who is doing better than us at something. But that says nothing about your fundamental worthiness as a human being. If that is never in question, then that gives you a core stability that renders you strong enough to use comparison to your advantage. When the slightest indication of not being the best yet is used as justification in your mind for the belief that you are worthless and doomed to inadequacy, it becomes impossible to work on yourself. The prospect of looking into the eyes of your own imperfections becomes too threatening and too painful. Performance is always workable, but worthiness is a constant.

Do not mistake self-worth for self-indulgence. In fact, it demands a complete lack of entitlement. The tendency to assume that good fortune has been simply gifted to others by the universe and the world owes you the same because you are worthy, too, is more likely to lead to bitterness and resentment rather than the action required to get you there.

To keep this work constructive and not let it dissolve into

global criticisms of the self, it requires that we ask questions like the following:

- What do I feel envious of specifically?
- What specific skills do they have that I would like to have also?
- Would learning those skills help me with achieving my own goals?
- How did they get there?
- Can I imitate any of that process to help me get closer to my personal goals?

This process turns envy into inspiration rather than a tool to hit yourself over the head with. Then comparison becomes a valuable part of the learning process.

Choosing your subject with precision

The most helpful upward comparison that inspires us to act on our goals is when we compare ourselves to individuals with a similar skill level in the discipline we are invested in mastering, rather than people who differ greatly from us.[3] That's another reason not to use social media for this. Even if the content is real, you are rarely looking at people who are in the middle of honing their craft. The algorithm throws you extremes, so you will be comparing yourself to the best in the world who are much further along their journey than you.

However momentarily inspiring or intriguing that may be, being bombarded with such extremes can be more likely to cause feelings of inferiority and depression rather than inspired learning of your next steps.[4] It can also lead to the justification of self-sabotage.[5] We zero in on extremes that seem so unattainably superior that we save ourselves from the discomfort of trying and failing to be the best.

If you notice you are making comparisons with extremes and feeling discouraged or disheartened by it, make a firm intention to seek out inspiration from someone just a few steps ahead. The boost you will experience from then achieving that will fuel your drive to keep working and improving.

From resentment to gratitude

Hand a child a treat, and see their face light up. Hand the child next to them two treats, and see the first child's face change to instant dissatisfaction with what they felt so pleased with just a moment ago. The risk of focusing on what others have that you don't is the creation of deep dissatisfaction with a life you could have loved. It no longer matters what I have, only that you have more. It is okay to want better for yourself, but if that comes from a place of resentment, then everything you achieve and accumulate will never feel enough. You will never get there. Your life will be marked by a repeated moving of the goalposts and shifting of whom you compare yourself to.

Resentment is not a reflection of what the world owes you. It is a sign of what you need to work on. You can see this as you look around at people who have more than most to be grateful for, but who are living in bitterness and resentment. This is something that can happen so easily when we make comparisons that don't serve us. If you are making comparisons that are not helpful to you, then you'll be wishing you had been dealt someone else's hand.

Listen to resentment. It might mean that you need to start putting in effort on your own behalf and speaking up for yourself. Or it might mean that you need to exercise gratitude by taking control of the focus of your attention in a way that serves you better.

Gratitude as a practice is often dismissed as too simple or insignificant. But if it was as easy as it sounds, there would be much less bitterness and resentment to witness. So strengthen your ability to turn your mind toward gratitude by making it a part of every day. Just two minutes each day reflecting on what you have to feel grateful for can be transformational and can remedy some of the damage done by unhelpful comparisons.

Why not immerse yourself in deep gratitude that you had the chance to see something wonderful achieved and that you live in a time when you have the freedom to work for something similar should you so wish? Deliberately find gratitude for the opportunity to try and the joy you can experience as you work on it. Doing this dissolves the need to match up to your comparison before you can feel satisfied with your life. In any case, we are comparing ourselves to people who are further along in their journey, so measuring success by our ability to catch up with them is not a good strategy. It keeps our own satisfaction with life always in the future, as we never reach the illusory destination. It forever remains somewhere up ahead.

Comparing downward is incredibly helpful for accessing a sense of gratitude. In the lowest of moments there is always something to be grateful for, but finding it can be difficult. So comparing your situation to the countless people who have it worse helps to shift that downward spiral and level off your perspective. (Unless you are using it to invalidate your own problems, which is less than helpful. Other people having it worse is not a good reason not to help yourself.)

"Resentment is not a reflection of what the world owes you. It is a sign of what you need to work on."

Reconnect with your values

If you are stuck in a pattern of destructive comparison, you will undoubtedly have lost touch with some of the things that matter most to you in your own life. When this happens, we look in the wrong places for a measure of ourselves.

We look out toward a world that is trying to sell us the fantasy that we would feel enough if only we had more stuff, extreme wealth, fame, and an appearance that can only be bought from a surgeon. This feeds more negative comparisons because the only way to know if you are keeping up with the Joneses is to examine them and see how you compare. Taking these marketing tools as your own values puts you at greater risk of depression, anxiety, addiction, narcissism, and the rest.[6] Don't wait to be told what matters to you. It doesn't take long to reconnect with the things that are guaranteed to bring a more deeply meaningful experience to your life.

I have placed exercises that help with this in the appendix (see page 293), partly because they are relevant to every one of life's problems. Knowing who you want to be before you look too deeply at others gives you a rudder to steer your life in the direction that best suits you.

The most useful comparison to you

The best comparison you can make is with yourself. Ask yourself if you have made today that tiny bit better than yesterday. This allows you to witness your own progression. But don't stop there. Next, take a look at the comparison between where you are now and where you want to be tomorrow, next month, and next year. Are you doing things today that are taking you in that direction? What does that tell you about the actions you need to take now?

If you trained yourself to notice when you were engaging in self-destructive comparisons and replaced them with comparison focused entirely on your own goals, imagine what you could achieve in just a year. Imagine how differently you could feel about yourself and your life. There is only one way to find out.

Takeaways

- If you compare yourself to someone else and come up short, either you feel inspired by what is possible and motivated to learn, or you fall into a downward spiral of dissatisfaction with your life and yourself. If your experience is the second one, then the problem is not you and all of your apparent inadequacies, it's your comparisons.

- It is never as easy as just deciding to stop comparing yourself. Your ability to do that is a built-in tool that is as helpful as it is dangerous. When used right, it can help steer you in the right direction, help inspire you, and help you push beyond your limits. When used in the wrong way, the damage it can do is far-reaching and long-lasting.

- Comparing yourself to people on social media or in your most cherished social circle will do damage to you and your relationships. When you notice yourself doing it, act fast and remind yourself of the essential components of helpful comparison.

- Keep any comparisons goal-specific and directed toward your own improvement and how you intend to get there.

- Keep self-worth out of it. This is not indulgence; it is necessary for learning.

- Choose someone whose current level of ability is a challenge but achievable with effort.

- When comparison has left you resentful, call a stop to it and turn back toward your own life, putting your energy into reconnecting with a sense of gratitude for everything that matters to you.

- Don't compare yourself to someone whose values do not reflect your own.

- Look at where you were yesterday to feel the thrill of your progress, and look at where you want to be tomorrow to keep you on course.

CHAPTER 2

When your friends are not your friends

Better an honest enemy than a false friend.

—German proverb

A letter from me to you

There are times in life when you start to feel differently about certain people. Maybe even friends you've had for years. Nothing big or dramatic may have happened, but you have this gut feeling that you're not entirely welcome here anymore. If that is you, then there are a few things to get straight in your mind.

First, we have an incredible tendency to ignore that gut feeling. You might not remember every detail of the occasional raised eyebrow or the praise that felt more like poison, you just know that you felt tense and on edge in their presence, not safe to be yourself. Maybe you notice that every time you see them you now come away feeling drained and wondering if they like you. These emotional imprints of the interaction can last longer than memory for the details, so don't discount how those people make you feel. It might not be the definitive answer to all your questions, but it is information not to dismiss.

Second, when a friendship is dependent on you bringing something other than yourself in order to be acceptable, that is not friendship. You might notice that, to be included, you have to keep your mouth shut about all the good things going on for you, since they appear to be seen as a threat by a particular person. You have to shrink down until you are small enough for them to tolerate. It's a risky business taking responsibility for someone else's ego in this way. It is essentially playing their game and losing every time just to have a chance to play again.

Third, when a so-called friend is treating you in a way that hurts you, it is not okay. And you do not have to suffer through that, even if you have been friends for years. You are not obliged to stay in a friendship that is not healthy for you. This is something that many of us battle with for years before we finally pluck up the courage to say enough is enough. We find ourselves fixed to the spot by a lifetime of greeting cards that tell us "friendship is forever." But not only are you free to choose your own friendships, you are also duty-bound to do the best for yourself, which includes making careful decisions about whom you spend your time with. It is not just friendship that is crucial to a healthy and fulfilled life, it is good-quality friendship.

Fourth, when a friend reveals themselves to you with anything along the lines of jealousy, contempt, or deceit, watch and learn.

If the sharing of a personal victory is met with dagger eyes and a dose of stonewalling, watch and learn.[1] And if the sharing of bad news is quickly minimized or one-upped by something "much worse" that happened to them years ago, squashing your bid for support as they fight for the spotlight, watch and learn. Learn to recognize those signs that someone does not have your best interests at heart.

Once they have proved themselves to be someone you cannot trust, you have a decision to make. And as you think about it, keep in mind that you cannot force anyone else to be a better friend. You can only control whom you spend your time with. But when the person who is treating you badly has been your friend for years, the story in your mind says, if I could just try a bit harder, be a little more this and a little less that, then maybe they would like me. Then I'd fit in. And maybe that's true. But do you want to fit in when the situation demands you be someone other than yourself? Fitting in is not the same as belonging. When you belong, it's because you are accepted exactly as you are.

Perhaps an essential part of the journey toward finding a sense of belonging is learning along the way that none of us can ever be liked by everyone. And if we don't trap ourselves with the idea that all friends are forever, then that becomes easier to accept and we're free to make different choices if a friendship turns out not to feel like friendship at all.

That doesn't make it easy to move on from old friends, even when their behavior is harmful to you. But surrounding yourself with people who bring out the worst in you or bring you down is not going to add to your life. It will only take away.

"Fitting in is not the same as belonging. When you belong, it's because you are accepted exactly as you are."

Real-time tools

According to greeting cards and slogans on mugs, true friendship lasts a lifetime, no matter what. But it's hard to square that with real life. It's normal to have ups and downs in friendship, but how do you know when a friendship no longer qualifies as a friendship at all? And when is it okay to say, this isn't for me? Of course, these are decisions that only you can make, so here are a few things to take into account as you reflect on them.

Deciphering the difference between constructive and cruel criticism

If your friend has become critical of your choices or actions, it is tempting to conclude that they are not a true friend. That stems from the assumption that friends should support us through everything. But that is also assuming that all the decisions you make are good ones. Many of us act out destructive patterns of behavior at some point in our lives and convince ourselves that we are doing the right thing. When a friend criticizes those actions, is it right to assume they are no friend of yours, end the friendship, and carry on? What if that friend has been a voice of reason that you have valued and respected over the years? What if there's more than one friend saying the same thing?

Friends are not there only to offer an echo chamber. But so many friends do this to each other. Through fear of offending or disrupting the friendship, they agree with things they know all too well sound like excuses or justifications. A true friend will remind you of your values when you seem to have lost your way. Wanting the best for you means calling you out on your poor decisions and being brave enough to have the uncomfortable conversation that encourages you to hold yourself accountable when you get into destructive patterns. It takes some courage and skill to disagree with and provide a reality-check for a friend who is not taking responsibility for their actions or is playing games with people. It always runs the risk of rejection because nobody wants to hear that they are not doing themselves proud. But there is a certain level of self-betrayal inherent in saying things you don't believe in order to keep the connection. That is not showing up as you truly are. It is acting out a particular version of yourself that feels acceptable to the other. Genuine friends can disagree yet still maintain love and compassion for each other. But if someone is not telling the truth, do you even really know each other?

Not all criticism is created equal. Some friends will come to you with painful but honest words aimed at helping you to keep sight of your values. Others will criticize to bring you down and to minimize whatever threat they see in you.

The time to start ignoring criticism is when it comes laced with contempt. When you start to realize that, despite having known each other for a long time, that person does not have your best interests at heart. When it is not clear, it's worth asking yourself honestly and gently, is this warranted? Could this help me do better? Or is this actually about them?

Deciding when enough is enough

Deep grief is always going to follow the ending of a friendship that was once special to you. Decisions to end friendships should not be made lightly, but with great thought and consideration. And there is no hard-and-fast rule that makes those decisions for you. For example, many viral one-liners spout that if a friend cannot celebrate your successes with you, ditch them, as they're not your friend. But how do you apply that to a more complex, real-life scenario? Imagine two friends: one is ten years into a fertility battle and the other gets pregnant. It would be rather self-absorbed to expect that first person to skip into a baby shower ready to celebrate. Life is full of situations like this one, marked with depth and complexity, that call for nuance in our approach, gentle compassion from both sides, and a difficult but crucial conversation about how to navigate all the very natural emotions that arise as we work hard to stay connected and look out for each other.

On the other hand, a friend who appears to quietly compete with you, talks negatively about you in your absence, and excludes or ignores you when you achieve positive things for your life is not likely to be a keeper. If you notice that you often feel good about yourself, but not in their presence, that's a feeling that needs listening to.

Fear of being alone

Holding on to a harmful or unhealthy friendship for fear of not having many other friends is normal but often can keep you unnecessarily trapped. This is similar to the way some people convince themselves to stay in destructive romantic relationships, overgeneralizing that, because this one hasn't worked out, no others will either. But, for the most part, the choice is not between unhealthy friendship and loneliness. The choice is between unhealthy friendship and a new (albeit scary) challenge to find other friends.

Staying in a damaging friendship to avoid loneliness is not a great strategy for your mental health in the long run. Good friendships are great for your well-being. Bad friendships, not so much. The point of friendship is not to drive you into the ground and diminish you. If your friends make it harder to stay mentally well, that's a sign not to ignore. A friendship that's more damaging to your life than restorative is not a friendship at all.

So keep in mind that the tendency to overgeneralize between this friendship and future ones is likely to keep you stuck rather than help you move forward.

Hold yourself to the same standards

In our tendency to focus on ourselves and what we want, need, and expect from friends, it is a healthy exercise to occasionally ask ourselves what *we* are bringing to the friendship. While the best of friends want the best for you, we should also want the best for them. If a good friend is slipping away, it makes sense to focus on what you can do to be a better friend and create a stronger bond. Ask yourself: Have I been keeping them at arm's length? Have I allowed myself to drift away, concerned with my own life? Have I been reaping the benefits of their support but can't remember the last time I listened to what they were going through? Is there anything I have been doing to create an atmosphere that holds people back from being unapologetically themselves around me?

This is not about turning on yourself and blaming yourself for the breakdown of a friendship. But if you are brave enough to account for the fact that you must both bring something to the table for the friendship to work, then you can be sure that you made a conscious effort to contribute fairly to the friendship.

Resist victimhood

Much of the heartbreak felt after betrayal by a friend is embedded in our natural tendency to take things personally. But keep in mind that this behavior will have much more connection to their relationship with themself and the unhealthy templates they have for relationships. Turning the whole thing inward and ruminating on the question "How could they do this to *me*?" leads only to a sense of victimhood and a rageful urge to get revenge or bring someone down. That pathway serves you in no way. To resist that slippery slope, always keep your options in view. However you respond to the situation you are in, make it a conscious choice and an exercise of your own agency.[2]

Allow all experiences, from the joyously positive to the downright heartbreaking, to be different lessons in a lifelong education about human relationships. As you move forward into the next chapter of your life, you get to choose whose stories will cross over with yours. If healing a friendship after a mistake or difficult time would be a chapter you want to include, then take control of that and tread carefully. Equally, if this particular character is taking the story to places you don't want to go, you might want to give them a smaller part.

Takeaways

- It's not just friendship that is so crucial to a healthy and happy life, it's good-quality friendship. People who call themselves friends but harm you with their behavior are not adding to your life, they are taking away from it.

- Whether it's the good news or the bad, if you have to keep parts of your life under wraps to fit in, that's not a friendship that is going to nourish and bring out the best in you.

- A good friend is not the one who continues to provide an echo chamber as you go on a downward spiral of bad life choices. A good friend will be brave enough to remind you of your values when you have lost your way on a self-destructive path. So criticism alone is not a reason to end a relationship. But criticism (or indeed praise) laced with contempt is a sign that this friend might not have your best interests at heart.

- Don't be ruthless in your decisions. This is your life. Be careful, considered, and deliberate. And if you do walk away from a friendship, do it with compassion. Wish them well and make sure that your decision is so well-thought-out that you take no bitterness with you.

- Let's always aim for balance. With all this focus on whether our friends are doing a good enough job, always be willing to reflect on whether you are bringing to your friendships and communities what you hope to receive.

CHAPTER 3

When you want to be less awkward around people

To be interesting, be interested.

—Dale Carnegie, *How to Win Friends and Influence People*

A letter from me to you

When a social interaction suddenly feels awkward, it is usually because you get distracted with concern for how you are coming across to the other person, which prevents you from fully absorbing yourself in the conversation. It's especially anxiety provoking if we don't believe that we have the ability to control that in the way we'd like.

The more that feeling arises, the more we start to see social interactions as something to be endured rather than enjoyed. The main aim becomes simply to escape without humiliation. Then, after the interactions, even the ones that went well, the rumination begins as you replay the conversations in your mind.

A storytelling about all the different negative judgments that must have been bestowed upon you in the moments when you dared to let your guard down and fully engage in the conversation. All of this makes social interaction a big event that must be prepared for and recovered from.

But shyness and a few awkward moments don't have to stop two people from developing a deep and fulfilling relationship. Both occur naturally. And both lose some of their power over us if we stop waiting for them to disappear and are willing to face them.

Telling yourself that you don't have the skills is not the end of the story. People spend a lifetime honing the craft of interacting with other humans. There is always more to learn, and during that process, you will discover that you can tolerate the discomfort of awkward moments here and there. You learn that the possibility of awkward moments happening doesn't disappear. You just become more confident that you will get through them. As you grow, the hurdle appears less of a problem. The only way to get to that place and uncover more of your potential is to walk through it.

As you enter interactions with people, spend less time worrying about what you might say and how to appear confident. Instead, make it your new mission to bring out positive things in the people around you. In the moments that you would previously have worried about whether you fit in, turn your attention to making sure that the people around you feel welcome, feel interesting, and feel a part of things. See if you can create an interaction that ends in the other person walking away feeling ten feet tall, feeling that someone was genuinely interested in knowing them.[1] When you manage to get even close to that, they will remember how you made them feel. Such interactions lead to much richer connections than if you focused on simply impressing them with social confidence. If it's about them, you don't need to be a social butterfly. You can show up exactly as you are.

Their response to feeling safe with you will undoubtedly be to do the same for you and consequently create a deeper connection between you both. Much of the time we are so focused on whether we feel we belong that we neglect to consider what others are experiencing, and our own power to do anything about that. We can craft a situation to nurture a sense of belonging for others, and when we do, we inadvertently start to feel it ourselves too.

Real-time tools

Endless articles and books have been written claiming to offer the secret to that one trick you can use to instantly feel confident when talking to other people. But building your social confidence is not just about what you do during the social interaction. The many ways in which we keep ourselves stuck in our social fears tend to show up before, during, and after the social interaction itself. There are tools included here that cover each of those bases.

Spot your own covert avoidance

When we feel anxious or awkward in a social setting, it's only natural to want to snatch small moments of recovery. Maybe we avoid the fear of starting a conversation by heading off to the bathroom or leaving early. Unsure of whom to speak to or what to say next, sometimes we stay in the room but seek the safety of a screen, looking down at the phone to avoid an awkward moment. But doing so can shut the door on other people looking for a friendly face. So focused on gaining relief from our own discomfort, we do not see the disinterest it portrays to others, who subsequently decide to give us space and not interrupt. Stuck in a feedback loop, we walk away feeling lonely and with added confirmation that people don't really want to know us.

The next time you find yourself in a social situation, see if you can go all in and resist the temptation to covertly avoid chances to interact.

It's not so much that the socially confident have worked out how to prevent awkward moments. It's much more that they barely focus on trying to avoid them at all. Instead, their focus is on having fun or getting to know certain people more deeply. Sometimes focusing only on what you are trying to avoid leads you straight to it. If all that is going through your mind is *Try not to look awkward, try not to say that wrong thing*, then before you know it you're blushing, your mind goes blank, and here comes the awkward silence you were so desperate to avoid.

Practice

The more time you spend alone, avoiding interaction, the more the fear response spikes when you have to interact with people. But while this shows you how we get stuck, it also shows us the way out. Habituation is the process by which your brain will downshift the stress reaction in response to repeated exposure. The more you can give yourself practice at social situations and resist the urge to seek safety through avoidance, the more your brain will calm the stress response. Your brain will learn from experience that this is not as dangerous as it once appeared to be. In the process, you will build on social skills and memories of fruitful interactions that felt positive.

"It's not so much that the socially confident have worked out how to prevent awkward moments. It's simply that they barely focus on trying to avoid them at all. Sometimes focusing only on what you are trying to avoid leads you straight to it."

The answer to overcoming those awkward moments and the social anxiety surrounding them is not to avoid social events but to see them as your chance to face those fears and practice the skills you pick up along the way. But you don't have to dive in at the deep end with the most terrifying social situations. Start as small and manageable as you like and build up gradually. The key is that you offer yourself the chance to have regular, positive experiences of social interaction.

Learn, don't compare

Watching others who interact well is a valuable exercise but only if you are doing so with the clear aim of learning from them. Shy people have a tendency to search for the most outstanding social butterfly and then compare themselves negatively and harshly, fueling beliefs that not being the heart and soul of the party is a fundamental inadequacy of character that is both innate and unchangeable. Once we are in the firm grip of this narrative, we become more self-conscious and more likely to try to escape and avoid rather than take chances to learn and develop our skills in the craft of social interaction.

Those comparisons are likely to give you the impression that you are alone in feeling awkward, a belief that research has shown us not to be true. At least 90 percent of college students report feeling shy at some point in their lives, and 48 percent of adults say they consider themselves shy.[2] At any given moment, around half the people in the room will be feeling a similar way, and the rest will have memories of feeling shy in the past. You are never truly alone in this very human experience. When you're scanning the room for signs of potential rejection, often what you are seeing is in fact signs of hesitation produced by shyness or anxiety.

Focus on feelings, not on words

When we feel shy or a little anxious, we get caught up in what to say and how to fill silences. But the solution to shyness or those awkward moments is not having a script to lean on. Creating connection with another person lies in the feelings we bring up in them. There are a thousand ways to make someone feel welcome and a little more at ease.

Anxiety tells us we must impress people and be accepted by them. But when connection is our goal, it calls for a humble focus on the person in front of you, an interest and appreciation for them. Aiming to help the other person feel safe requires a gentle, honest, and trustworthy approach. Concentrating on the ways in which you can contribute to creating an environment that helps others to feel wanted, accepted, cared for, and interesting gives you an outward focus that mutes the self-conscious thoughts. You cannot give both your full attention, so use your new mission to ease your worry about how you're coming across.

Put a stop to the post-social rumination

Even when a social interaction goes well, the shy or anxious have a tendency to engage in a little post-social rumination. We replay moments of the conversation and try to imagine what the other person was thinking, how they might have been judging us. We punish ourselves for the slightest of awkward moments with a heavy dose of self-blame, and slip into despair at the possibility that those other people will forever judge us from now on.

Such rumination offers nothing positive for you. It will worsen your mood as well as your anxiety. Normalize the awkward moments, and rather than punish yourself with this self-flagellation, reward the effort you made to engage and keep reminding yourself of the value in each and every social dance, even the ones where you stumble and tread on your partner's toes. The moment is over, so move on to the next.

Challenge the spotlight effect

Something we all do is overestimate how much others are noticing us and scrutinizing or judging us negatively. Because we are the center of our own world, we wrongly assume we are close to the center of everyone else's. But the reality is that most people are cross-examining their own social performance, rather than ours. That doesn't mean you are invisible to them or that they do not care; it just means they are not thinking as deeply or critically about your insecurities as you are. They have plenty of their own to battle.

When this bias is in action, we are prone to the common but less than helpful coping strategy of sitting back and hoping that the social butterflies will come and take us under their social wings. We buy into the narrative that if we can present ourselves as perfect enough, if we look right and say things right, then others will do the rest of the work, putting themselves on the line to initiate social interactions and bring us out of our shells. But doing this reinforces the biased thought that everyone is looking at us and judging, and that if nobody connects with us, it was because we didn't appear perfectly. It also creates anxiety by handing over control to others and expecting them to create a positive social interaction for us. Creating a sense of agency over our social interactions involves taking on the responsibility of putting in the work, initiating new interactions, and investing the energy to develop them further.

When you notice yourself imagining that everyone is focusing on you and judging, remind yourself how inaccurate we know this to be and how unhelpful it is for you to give it your time and attention. Notice it as a manifestation of the stress response kicking off and your brain's attempt to keep you safe in your social world. When we can thank the mind for making us aware of the worst-case scenarios and then choosing not to fight with those thoughts and not to engage with them or believe in them as facts, then we are free to look at other ways of perceiving this situation that hold more value or utility.

Search for smiles, not scowls

As you enter a social situation, telling yourself the water is full of sharks and then scanning for them will make the slightest flutter of the smallest fish look like a threat. Instead, as you look toward others, and as you listen to them, search their words, not for coldness, but for connectedness. Find ideas and experiences and values that you share.[3] This does not have to be intimidating. In fact, this is where small talk paves the way for connection. If you can agree on your thoughts about the weather as you enter the room, then the proverbial ice is already broken. Finding common ground, however small at first, can give you both a boost that sets a conversation in motion. There is nothing that gets two strangers smiling at each other more than finding out they once lived in the same town, visited the same holiday destination, knew the same person, or are simply able to laugh together. All of these seemingly small or superficial moments are in fact potent at dissolving those initial inhibitions and allowing us to build momentum in our conversation.

Takeaways

- When a social interaction suddenly feels awkward, it is usually because you get distracted with concern for how you are coming across to the other person, which prevents you from being fully absorbed in the conversation. It's especially anxiety provoking if we don't believe that we have the ability to control these impressions in the way we'd like.

- As you enter interactions with people, spend less time worrying about what you might say and how to appear confident. Instead, make it your new mission to bring out those things in the people around you. In the moments when you would previously have worried about whether you fit in, turn your attention to making sure that the people around you feel welcome, interesting, and a part of things.

- It's not so much that the socially confident have worked out how to prevent awkward moments. It's simply that they barely focus on trying to avoid them at all. Instead, their focus is on having fun or getting to know certain people more deeply. Sometimes focusing only on what you are trying to avoid leads you straight to it.

- The answer to overcoming those awkward moments and the social anxiety surrounding them is not to avoid social events but to see them as your chance to face those fears and practice the skills you pick up along the way.

- Put a stop to the post-social rumination.[4] It will only bring down your mood and heighten your anxiety. Congratulate yourself for making the effort to face those fears and, whether the experience was positive or not, move on to the next.

- When you're interacting with people, search their words, not for coldness, but for connectedness. Find ideas and experiences and values that you share.

CHAPTER 4

When you feel unwelcome and want to fit in

To be yourself in a world that is constantly trying to make you something else is the greatest accomplishment.

—Ralph Waldo Emerson

A letter from me to you

Every time we step into a space with other people, we ask ourselves: Do I belong here? We scan the room for a friendly face and wait politely to be welcomed. So fundamental is the need to be secure as a member of a group that your brain continues to assess it, even when you've known your friends for years. We are so attuned to our place in a group that just the raising of a brow or the rolling of eyes can set those alarm bells ringing and put you on edge.

If you find yourself feeling unwelcome or questioning whether you belong, you might be tempted to adjust yourself to fit in.

There is nothing wrong with that, and we all do it in small ways every day. But you are also making an assumption about the value of this group. What happens when your acceptance is conditional on you lying about what you believe to be true? Or maybe being a part of the group demands that you do things you're uncomfortable with and pretend to be someone you're not? This type of situation starts to feel less like belonging and much more like manipulation.

This primary driving force to attach to others is so pervasive that we often don't stop to ask ourselves: Is this somewhere that I want to belong? If you run the risk of being excluded for the slightest of blunders, was that ever a group that could offer a true and deep sense of belonging? Is that a group anyone can feel safe in? More likely, you will spend your days scanning for signs of disapproval from others and people-pleasing your way into becoming an anxious wreck.

Asking these questions can be life altering when it opens our eyes to the choice laid out in front of us and the realization that we don't need to belong everywhere and don't need acceptance from everybody. But what happens when the answer is "Yes, I do very much want to belong here"? Then the next step is not to walk away but to find a way to connect with the people in this group.

Whether we are usually socially anxious or not, when we enter a situation in which we are unsure of whether we are welcome, our threat system is very much alert to that. Our natural response to uncertainty is to hold back and assess the situation. So we hover on the fringes for a while, hoping that someone will engineer a sense of belonging for us so that we can relax. But when we do this, we forget that most other people are looking for the same thing from us. Everyone is looking to each other to meet their need to feel welcome. And holding back does not create that for anyone in the group.

So many people will tell you that in these moments you must have the courage to stand alone. But a focus that I have found more life-changing is having the courage to connect. When we shift our focus away from how we want others to make us feel and instead pay attention to what we can offer them, you immediately inject a sense of agency into the situation. You no longer have to be consumed with worries about whether you are being welcomed enough or whether others are bothering to connect. You are the welcomer. You are taking on the responsibility of making a connection.

Making that decision to first give what you wish to receive and to take responsibility for creating those connections, even in the moments when you feel out of place, can feel pretty radical when our natural human instinct is to wait for others to take control of the situation. But I dare you to try it. Walk into a room with a mission to make others feel welcomed by you. Take a genuine interest in each individual without the expectation of anything in return and see what happens.

Real-time tools

Our sense of connection both at home and in our institutions is a big predictor of mental health.[1] So what better tools to practice using than the ones that help us increase our ability to create connections? For many people, honing this craft might also include tackling social anxiety, learning communication skills, and undergoing assertiveness training. But included here are the real-time tools that you can try in the moment when you want to take on a new sense of agency in social situations.

Search in the right places

The very first consideration here needs to be whether this is a good place for you to seek some form of acceptance and belonging. Many of us look for belonging in the wrong places. We have deep-rooted core beliefs about who we are and what we deserve. We don't consciously think about these day to day. But if our template for the world shapes us as someone who is unlovable and inadequate, and will never amount to much, then it's possible that we will feel undeserving of belonging in groups that might challenge those beliefs. Instead, we seek acceptance in groups that reinforce that low opinion of ourselves and that keep us stuck.

While we cannot eliminate our need to feel that we belong, we can make careful choices about where we search for acceptance. If you feel unwelcome in a group, it is always an option to ask yourself:

- Is this a place I truly want to belong?
- Would being recognized as a part of this group be a positive in my life?
- How much of myself, my beliefs, or my values would I be expected to change in order to be accepted? Is that okay with me?

Search for what you want to find

If you enter a situation with a sense of foreboding, anticipating that disapproval or rejection must be coming, then your brain will do its job to keep you safe. It will scan that room for any signs of threat. And when you search, you find.

When our focus is on protecting ourselves from potential judgment or rejection, we hold back. "The less you fully know me, the less you can hurt me." But keeping people at arm's length causes them to question how we feel toward them. They, too, are looking for cues that they are safe in our company. So what starts off as self-protection only serves to stunt the connection. When they distance themselves in response to our seeming lack of enthusiasm toward them, it is their own form of self-protection based on the cues we have given them.

The writer David Brooks puts it perfectly in his book *How to Know a Person*: "A person who is looking for beauty is likely to find wonders, while a person looking for threats will find danger." Remembering that your attention is like a spotlight and that you have control of it changes the game in social interactions. Feeling welcome and accepted is a function of the connection that we make with people. And the connection we make is not out of our hands. It is often determined by how much we approach a person with genuine curiosity, helping them to feel valued and interesting in the way that we would like to feel ourselves. For this, your attention must be on finding out about their life and what matters to them.

If anxiety makes it difficult to think of new questions, it is perfectly okay to prepare a few questions to fall back on. But the key is to remain genuinely curious about the person in front of you as someone worth knowing. When that is your focus, the conversation will develop naturally and they will feel welcomed by you.

Shift your focus and take the responsibility

Don't wait to be welcomed. Be the welcomer.

This is a conscious shift from a risk-avoidant mindset to an approach mindset. You go from a stunned, rabbit-in-the-headlights feeling to a proactive and intentional mode, in which you have a strong sense of agency and a clear agenda.

If your focus is simply to avoid rejection, you will spend your time trying to remain invisible and likely feel disconnected from everyone.

When you assign yourself the responsibility of creating connections and helping others to feel welcomed, you don't need a set prescription for your every move. In each interaction and with every choice to act, think, and speak, you can simply ask yourself: Am I creating distance or cultivating closeness?

This is a distinct shift, especially for people who experience social anxiety. They typically show an inward focus, constantly questioning how they are perceived and whether they are being accepted. When we do this, we feel entirely at the mercy of the group and others' judgments. We start to question our worth if the group is not welcoming. We search the faces for a glimpse of kindness and the possibility of connection, rather than being the caring face that invites others to feel welcome. In a group full of people who need to feel welcome, who is taking responsibility for doing the welcoming? Of course, taking the lead in this way involves vulnerability. Some will accept your invitation for connection, others might not. So we cannot measure our own self-worth on the reactions of all the people we attempt to interact with. I could fill several books with all the different possible reasons that someone might not respond to a bid for connection that have nothing to do with the person who initiated it. Taking it personally is a biased thought process that will only steer you further from your ambitions to become more socially confident.

Find common ground

If we are to focus on how we can create a sense of belonging in others, knowing fully that this is what everyone is seeking, how do we even begin to do this?[2]

When you question whether you can belong in a group and your brain is frantically searching for signs that you are different and inadequate compared to this group, you magnify anything that separates you from these people. Before you have even joined a conversation, you feel different and detached, neglecting all the information that shows we are more the same than we are different. Finding even the slightest of common ground can remedy that. I think this is what people are doing when they talk about the weather or complain about traffic. We don't know each other yet, but we all arrived here in the rain, so let's connect on that for a moment and break the psychological ice. You often see comedians establish a rapport with their audience by making a few jokes about the town they're performing in. It's a common ground, a basis for connection. "Here is something we both have an experience of, however mundane." These subtle but beautiful moments open the gate and say "Come in, you're welcome here."

So the next person you meet, aim to find similarities, nothing more. Maybe they have visited the town you live in, or you both got stuck in the same traffic this morning. Maybe you both have children or dislike the buffet. The details are not important. It's the moment of connection that results.

"Don't wait to be welcomed. Be the welcomer."

Takeaways

- We did not choose our common need for belonging, but we can choose where we look for it. If you are about to start adjusting who you are to fit in, is this a place you truly need and want to belong?

- In moments of social uncertainty we are often told to have the courage to stand alone. But better outcomes for everyone are possible when we have the courage to connect.

- Look for the best in people and that is what you will find. Look for the worst and you will find that too. Focusing on all the judgment you want to avoid will stunt the connection, not create it.

- Rather than concentrating on whether others will make you feel welcome, be the welcomer and see what happens.

- To ignite connection, find some common ground. No matter how small or insignificant, it will lay the foundation for connection.

CHAPTER 5

When you keep saying yes but you want to say no

When you say "yes" to others, make sure you are not saying "no" to yourself.

—Paulo Coelho

A letter from me to you

If you find it impossible to say no to other people, even when you most need to, then this is something to take very seriously indeed. Being able to stand up for yourself and say no is one of the most fundamental skills that you are going to need in your life. Many people are taught that being a good person equates with being nice, making sure that everybody else around you feels comfortable and gets their needs met. But being able to say no to the right things is at the very core of being a good person.

If your focus is on being the nice person in every situation you face, then the potential for your actions to be good will always be at the mercy of the whims and ideology of the person you're conceding to. Being a good person does not mean following what others think or waiting to be told what you have permission to do and how to do it. Being a good person is much, much harder than that. It demands that you think for yourself about right and wrong so deeply that your morals cannot easily be pushed aside for someone else's feelings.

There will be times in your life when there will be no one in your corner. You will have to fight alone. Maybe you will be negotiating for yourself or maybe for a loved one who can't do it for themselves. Either way, you are going to need the tools to stand up for yourself and make your voice heard so that you're not simply railroaded by someone else who did learn how to advocate for themselves and whose self-worth is not predicated on always being the "nice person."

Now, when you realize that you have a lot to learn in this area of your life, the tendency might be to use it as a stick to beat yourself with: a weapon of self-loathing. But taking responsibility for the feelings of others is not a character flaw that needs eradicating. It's not as simple or as ruthless as that. In fact, if you're a naturally agreeable person, those traits are a huge strength when it comes to things like parenting small infants. This is when your sensitivity to the feelings of others becomes your superpower and will help you create a secure bond that is absolutely necessary for that baby to thrive. Or maybe the tendency to appease the people around you was a survival strategy in a tough childhood. Either way, my point here is that your agreeableness should not be seen as a weakness. However, it does mean that you will need to arm yourself with the courage and the skills to advocate for yourself once in a while. Without doing that, adult relationships will prove dangerous.

You might think dangerous is an overly dramatic term. But saying yes when you want to say no will see you compromising not only your preferences and needs, but also what you know to be right and true. Once you start to edge over that line, denying your own judgment and fundamentally betraying yourself to please someone else, then everything starts on a downward spiral.

Your estimation of yourself gets chipped away by all of those small self-betrayals that, at the time, seem like no big deal. After all, what is one tiny crack in a dam? And if we tolerate one without too much damage, why not tolerate another, and another? A relationship tends not to switch from healthy to damaging overnight. We relinquish our hand one card at a time.

How do you know if you're heading in that direction? Well, maybe you say "I don't mind" much more than you say "yes" or "no." Maybe you absorb everyone else's preferences, needs, and beliefs so much that you're not sure you have many of your own anymore. Maybe your expression of yourself swells and shrinks to fit the space that is given to you. But any time you are unwilling or unable to say no, you instantly relinquish your power in the interaction. If you don't have the power to assert yourself so that you can live in line with what you believe to be right or even simply to protect your physical and mental health, then you will be vulnerable to being manipulated or exploited, and even your own sense of morality will be easily crumbled in the hands of the people you can't tell no.

This letter is so much more than me simply telling you to find the courage and sometimes say no for a happier life. I am saying that you cannot begin to imagine how unrecognizable you will become to yourself if you don't start working on this now.

Saying no, not only when it is easy, but when it is right, will do so much more for you than just keep you and your relationships healthy. It will, at times, be your only protection from forces outside yourself that would otherwise easily manipulate you into becoming a person you don't like and don't want to be.

Please never assume that feeling unable to say no doesn't matter. It matters for both you and the people in your life. And the good news is that the more you work on this, the braver you become and the more your life starts to reflect your own choices and intentions rather than just everyone else's.

It is not fair to you or any other person to hand them the compass for your life and leave it to chance that the direction they take will be right for you. Every little wrong turn they make along the way starts to make you feel victim to their choices. You must have your own compass and a clear sense of direction for the kind of person you want to be and why. Then it is so much easier to see what you need to say yes to and what you need to say no to.

Real-time tools

The dilemma of when to push for what you want and when to override it for others is deeply confusing in the moment, partly because the emotions driving this are created not just from the present but also from the past.[1] It is not as simple as switching out a yes for a no. Those strong emotions pull you in different directions like opposing tides. So wherever you are, you can't seem to feel comfortable.

Learning to say no requires a good dose of courage to deal with those emotions that pull us in these different directions and some solid assertiveness skills, so let's go through some of the real game changers from the literature that will help you along the way.

Dealing with the guilt of saying no

When it comes to all those emotions that make saying no so much harder than it sounds, one of the biggest players here is guilt. Saying yes when we need to say no is an emotional trade-off. We don't want to carry the guilt, so we back down, and that small dose of resentment that we're left with feels like a more manageable price to pay—for a while. But every time we trade guilt for resentment, the weight of that resentment gets a little heavier. It doesn't dissolve and it doesn't disappear. It grows and spawns bitterness and bouts of rage that seem to come out of nowhere. And the more it grows over time, the harder it becomes to hide it both from yourself and the people in your life. You might say, you become quite difficult to be around. If you don't ever make your case or stand for what you want, everyone around you is left guessing, and when they get it wrong, the resentment starts to leak out, and this air of misery and bitterness permeates so that even those you were trying to put first start feeling resentful toward you.

But how do you say no without feeling guilty? The short answer is: you don't have to. If you know a decision is the best one to make, you can take the guilt with you. Feelings are a great source of information, but they don't have all the facts. So listen to their suggestions, but remember who is in the driver's seat. You don't have to eliminate feelings of guilt before you move on. If you are willing to take it with you, it won't hold you back.

If you know that you feel guilty every time you say no, even when saying no is the right thing to do, practicing mindfulness can really strengthen that ability to notice the feeling and get some distance from it, a bird's-eye view. We can notice all those urges to relinquish control and succumb, but at the same time recognize that we get to choose whether we act on those urges or instead do something different, depending on what's right for us. If you would like guided mindfulness meditations to help get you started, I have some that you can access for free on my You-Tube channel (@DrJulie).

Update the meaning of those emotions

Feelings are not just generated from the present moment. They are also echoes of the past. There was a time in your life when doing whatever made the adults around you happy and seeking their approval helped you to maintain your attachment to them. In your early years, that attachment was paramount and superseded every other need. It made absolute sense back then. In adult relationships, that guilt can feel almost reflexive and still arises whenever you bring your own needs into the equation. But while that might once have been a sign of danger, its meaning might need updating to signify something positive. Rather than accepting defeat, you are making a stand, looking after yourself, asserting your needs, advocating for yourself, and facing conflict.

Learn to fear your own disapproval more than theirs

When we are learning how to stand up for ourselves, other people are a big part of the equation. We want so much for them to like us, to think we are good and worth having around. But we are also afraid of abandonment, and if we think there is any chance of losing someone who matters to us, then we will place their opinion of us above our own. The narrative sounds something like, "As long as I make sure that everyone around me is okay and pleased with me, I will feel safe in that connection. As long as they approve of me, it matters less whether I do." When saying no brings up thoughts about not being a good person in the eyes of another, it can be linked to our agreeable nature but might also be the result of a learning experience in early life. That learning needs updating just like the meaning we attach to the guilt.

It is okay to fear someone else's disapproval, but you must fear your own more. There will always be people in your life whose opinions you value, but when it comes to your own life choices, the buck stops with you, and so your own values must be the anchor that determines whether you take off in this direction or that.

With that said, it's not as easy as simply waking up in the morning and convincing yourself to seek your own approval and care a little less about what others might be thinking. To build a sense of self that is more than holes in a sponge waiting to be filled by the overflow of others, you must take action. You must break routines, try new things, put yourself in situations to discover how you emerge, make connections, or return to things that were once a part of your life merely because you enjoyed them. You don't become the person you want to be by just thinking about it. You do it by living it. With that in mind, learning to stand up for yourself even when you fear rejection must include a commitment to take care of yourself in the face of it. So much of the drive to say yes when we need to say no is the deep-rooted fear of abandonment. It is a safety behavior, if you like. Building on your life and your sense of self in turn builds your confidence that you could survive abandonment. Until then, holding healthy boundaries will feel more fearful than it needs to be.

Explore how saying no could change things

When you are so used to saying "I don't mind" as a blanket response for all options presented to you, it's easy to lose a sense of yourself as a person with preferences and to envisage what life might be like if you advocated for them. So take some time to build that insight.

 Try this: If you don't have a clear idea of what you're aiming for, you are much less likely to get there. So take some time to cultivate a picture of what you're working toward by writing out detailed answers to the questions below.

Let's imagine that you spent a day going about your various tasks and interactions with the firm belief that your own preferences, values, and principles were valid in equal measure to everyone else's. For the whole day you committed to not trampling on your own needs.

- What would that look like?
- In real, concrete terms, what would you do differently?
- Where would the word *no* appear that it hasn't so far?
- Where would you need the most courage?
- What would you stand to lose and what would you stand to gain?
- Now, imagine you did that successfully every day. After one year, how might life look different for you?
- How would the people in your life also benefit?

When "no" is not heard

Are you not saying no, or are they not accepting no for an answer? If it is the latter, then that person is breaching your boundaries. Looking at your own role in this is the key to change. Assuming that the behavior of others is simply neutral is a mistake. Be alert to signs of manipulation that will make it harder for you to hold healthy boundaries and trap you in a position that feels powerless. Here are a few to look out for:

- Lying, making excuses, and blaming you for things they are responsible for.
- Withholding inconvenient truths and sharing only the parts of the truth that fit their agenda.
- Gaslighting. This is a form of manipulation that causes a person to start questioning their own perception of reality and doubting their own judgment, creating a

dependency on the gaslighter, who presents themselves as the best or only source of truth.

- Passive-aggressive behavior.
- Acts of kindness that have strings attached and are used later to sway your decisions on things.
- They slip into a victim role, casting you as rescuer, appealing to your compassion and sense of duty toward them. Refusing to take care of themselves if you don't do it for them.
- When you try to assert your own needs, they may step into that victim role and portray you as perpetrator. "How dare you suggest that you have needs. You think you have it bad? Here's a list of all the things that make it worse for me."
- Not being clear about what they want, and playing on your emotions, whether it be guilt, anxiety, or your sense of obligation.
- Constant criticism wrapped in "I love yous" and the suggestion that they are doing things for your own good, so you shouldn't take it so personally.
- Pushing you into all-or-nothing thinking. It's either your needs or theirs. The implication is that when you are caring about your own needs, you stop caring about theirs.

If you spot some of these signs, that's not a reason to give up on asserting yourself; it means you need to get very familiar with the assertiveness skills at your disposal, and practice them and refine your ability to discern which relationships are healthy and which relationships are dependent on you having no needs, preferences, or capacity to advocate for yourself.

"It is okay to fear someone else's disapproval, but you must fear your own more."

Assertiveness skills

If you are going to start advocating for yourself in a more successful way, then arming yourself with the relevant communication skills is the way forward.[2] This is one of the most valuable forms of skills acquisition that happens in therapy, and if you can access a clinician to help you work on it, then you can benefit from regular reflection on how that new learning is going down in your real life and how to pull yourself back in line when you might slip into old habits.

Assertiveness is much more than just how to communicate. It's also about developing such clarity of mind around your values, goals, and vision of who you want to become that it's much easier to know what you want in different situations and why. It becomes easier to understand when to let something go and when to summon the courage to stand up for yourself.

First of all, spend some time sharpening your vision of what matters to you and how you want to conduct yourself in your relationships and the rest of your life, centered on your personal values. I have included a guide for doing this in the appendix (see page 301).

Once you have set out what you are aiming for, then you can listen to the feelings that come up to signal when you need to stand up for yourself but perhaps have the urge to back down. You can tally up the feelings about this situation with the clear set of values you intend to live by. That will help to guide your decisions and prevent you from being railroaded by the need to appease others.

When you do decide to speak up for yourself, if it's not in the immediate moment, take the time to prepare the most articulate argument you can come up with. Write down what you are asserting and all the reasons why. When you're preparing what to say, hold back on judgment or blame that could stir up defensiveness in the other person. Keep in mind, this is not a battle of aggression. You probably don't want to damage the relationship. Overt aggression by way of exploding and yelling and making demands is likely to do that. But passive aggression will also do damage. So avoid any veiled aggression that might show up in sarcasm or the silent treatment. Let them know that you have their needs and wishes in mind too. But hold firm to the decision you've come to and why.

Here's a quick checklist for communicating assertively:

1. Try to state your understanding of the situation with as much neutrality and objectivity as possible to avoid pushing the other person into a defensive position.

2. It is okay to include how you feel about it, but stay very specific to the situation and to concrete behavior. Don't be tempted to start generalizing about how "this always happens" or making sweeping statements about the other person's character. So rather than "I hate how you always . . ." try saying, "When you do X, it makes me feel Y."

3. When you are saying no, don't tiptoe around the issue. Cut to the chase and be as clear and precise as you can possibly be.

4. When you get a positive response and the other person makes adjustments or respects your position, show good grace and gratitude in return. This will go a long way to reinforcing that behavior in the future.

5. If their response is not so positive and they persist in trying to encroach on the boundary you've asserted or they start insulting you and trying to shout you down, stay focused. This is when the broken-record technique comes in. Hold on to your prepared lines and don't be afraid to repeat them as much as you need.

6. Whether you have a prepared script or not, how you present yourself is paramount. Look that person in the eyes calmly, stand with confidence, and speak firmly but without aggression. If you enter that space as a shrinking violet or if you explode into a shouting, messy rage, you will be sacrificing the effectiveness of your own argument and will be much less likely to achieve what you want.

7. If you see a compromise that suits you both, it's okay to take it. But be sure that it does suit you both. If an apparent compromise would leave you resentful, then you're probably leaving the negotiation too early.

Takeaways

- There is a damaging misconception that being a nice person means giving in to other people's demands, always being the one to say "I don't mind," and flexing this way and that to accommodate everyone around you. But for anyone who aspires to live as what they deem to be a "good person," then assertiveness is the only way to do that. Without it, you'll be pulled in any direction life takes you.

- There will be times in your life when you will need to stand up for yourself or someone you love and won't have anyone else to lean on. You will need both the courage to advocate for yourself and the skills to negotiate with others who are not so worried about whether anyone considers them nice. The good news is that those skills can be mastered with practice.

  When you first start practicing assertiveness, saying no will be coupled with feelings of guilt. But that guilt can be an echo from the past. It does not automatically indicate that saying no was the wrong thing to do. If the decision is in line with your values, you can override the feelings that belong in the past.

- Avoiding potential conflict often feels like the easier option when you need to stand up for yourself or to say no. But taking that easier option chips away at you, and the fallout comes later.

- A big part of the challenge is to break through the indecision and the reluctance to face the potential conflict head-on.

- Assertiveness is often seen as just communication skills. But one of the hardest parts about advocating for yourself is knowing when to use them. Once you are armed with the tools, you need clarity on who you want to be in your relationships and your community. Then it becomes easier to understand when to let something go and when to summon the courage to hold your ground.

- A lifetime habit of appeasing others won't vanish overnight. There will be times when you recognize the need to stand up for yourself but have strong urges to back down. In those moments you can be railroaded before you have time to think about the set of values you intend to live by. Sometimes you'll surprise yourself and spontaneously use your new skills. Other times you'll repeat old patterns. They are not losses if you are willing to use them as a learning experience. Reflect on what made it difficult this time and how you could overcome that next time. Doing that will help to guide your decisions in similar situations that come up in the future.

CHAPTER 6

When you're dealing with passive-aggressive people

No one can make you feel inferior without your consent.

—Eleanor Roosevelt

A letter from me to you

"Well done on all of your success. You always were the over-achiever, weren't you." Ouch. What starts off sounding like tender praise from a friend suddenly tastes slightly off, injected with a subtle dig that lingers under your skin for days. Something so easily shrugged off as just a joke feels almost impossible to even question. So you're left wondering how this friend truly feels about you. A straightforward slap in the face would have been a much easier message to decipher.

Passive aggression can come from any angle, and that's because, let's face it, everyone dabbles in it occasionally. It is essentially human to use immature and unwise approaches to communication before we know better. A few backhanded comments from someone you don't know that well creates discomfort, but nothing makes you feel quite as cast out and alone as passive aggression that comes from someone you previously believed had your back. The visceral moment when you become aware that they want to see you suffer and squirm just a little. Or that a moment of one-upmanship means more to them than your relationship. The painful moment that shines a light on the sweet veil of smiles and you catch a glimpse of bitter intent behind it. Such a move punctures your view of that person and trust starts leaking out in a way that can't quite be repaired.

Experiencing passive aggression stings for sure. But don't be too distracted by the pain. Take a step back and bring the wider picture into view. There is much to be learned from this experience and all the others that come after it. This will not be the last time you encounter someone who uses indirect aggression to communicate, so let's make sure you take some of that learning with you to arm yourself for the future. Let's get so competent at dealing with underhanded behavior that we can anticipate these moves and can respond to them with a knowing smile, never thrown from our own objective or weakened by the temptation to drop to this level and fight it out. No need to be intimidated by this form of aggression or intimidate others with our own. No need to lose our heads in the scramble for victimhood. No. This power game is unwinnable and so participating only diminishes you.

Engaging in social scraps with people who are demonstrating that they do not have your back is a distraction from the much bigger and more important goals you have for yourself.

Take the learning to be had about dealing with such people, and once you've extracted what's useful, leave the encounter behind. Do not let it fester with the temptation to ruminate over it. Do not give the spotlight to the self-doubt that their tactics induced. That has a tendency to rot your self-confidence. Those feelings of uncertainty and insecurity arrived because that is exactly what passive aggression is intended to do. The feelings are a reflection of their behavior, not your apparent inadequacy.

Real-time tools

Sometimes you don't notice how dark it's become until someone switches a light on. Similarly, when someone starts to behave in a passive-aggressive manner, it can be difficult to work out why you suddenly feel on edge and alone. The first part of this tools section covers some of the ways it can show up. It also covers reasons people use such an approach with other people. Understanding why this might happen is not to justify it but to help us resist the urge to take it personally. Passive aggression has such potent effects on creating self-doubt in its target that our ability to hold the situation at arm's length and see the behavior for what it is holds the key to our resilience and to finding the response that will be most helpful.

How to identify passive aggression

Passive aggression is not always easy to spot but is most felt in the visceral impact it has. An impact that was intended. Ease gives way to tension, angst, and confusion about what just changed. On the surface everything appears fine, but you suddenly feel a little less safe. The person you assumed wanted the best for you subtly casts doubt. Maybe there's a slight whiff of hostility because their smile doesn't quite match how their words are making you feel.

Or perhaps you suddenly feel that you're no longer on the same team. There is a scoreboard between you. You're being competed against in a game you didn't know you were playing. You realize that you've hit the limits within which you are acceptable to this person. You walked into it like a glass door you couldn't see from back there. Everything was fine between you, until it wasn't. They were not satisfied with the dynamic and impulsively kicked out to rebalance things. They regain the upper hand without ever admitting to losing it. They might even slip into the role of victim like falling into a comfy chair after a long day, and it's your job to guess where you went wrong. If you're rattled by this, they instantly feel more significant and win that round.

You can spot passive-aggressive behavior when someone's negative emotion is being expressed indirectly in a form of muted hostility.[1] Here are a few telltale signs to look out for:

- Backhanded remarks
- Sarcasm
- Praise laced with insults
- Purposefully not following through on a contribution they had agreed to
- Sulking, becoming cold and indifferent
- Subtly excluding you from the social circle
- Engaging in gossip or sowing seeds of doubt in others about your character

- Agreeing to do something while making it clear that they definitely don't have the time or inclination or that it will cause them hassle
- Subtle comments in a superficially friendly interaction that chip away at your self-esteem and leave you doubting yourself and questioning how people really feel about you

When communication looks like this, it's likely that envy, jealousy, or some other uncomfortable emotion is not far under the surface.

Does this end a friendship?

Everyone engages in their fair share of passive-aggressive moves as they develop. The distinction lies between those who mature as they age and those who don't. A few cold words in a moment of weakness is something to be brushed off. A pattern that continues to repeat itself starts to shift a friendship or relationship from healthy and fulfilling to detrimental.

For those with a tendency toward covert narcissism, the passive-aggressive style of communication and the casting of self as victim are a classic trademark.[2] The general storyline might sound something like, "My life is harder than everybody else's and you should feel guilty about that. You should never ask me for more or go against my expectations of you. If you do, then you become the perpetrator in my story of victimhood." Unwritten rules like these are not conducive to a healthy relationship.

Understanding why they do it

Taking time to consider why someone is behaving this way toward you is a helpful part of the process in dealing with it. The reason is that the uncertainty and self-doubt seeded by passive aggression causes you to question if it's your own fault, when it's more likely to be reflective of their own patterns of relating to others. Understanding it is not justifying or validating it in any way. It is helping you get distance and see it for what it is—about them, not you.

In all honesty, the reason people use passive aggression is because, so much of the time, it works. And those we hurt feel unable to hold us to account for it. Nobody teaches us how to deal with difficult people. But in reality it robs both parties of the chance to communicate in a way that could resolve the issue. The passive-aggressive person drains their zest for life, leaking resentment from every weak point, and the other person wastes time and energy trying not to break the eggshells they are forced to walk on.

When we behave in a passive-aggressive way, it is often born out of a strong and highly uncomfortable emotion coupled with a sense of powerlessness to change it by expressing it openly and directly. For example, let's say you enjoyed a degree of social status among your friends. Perhaps you earned more or were regarded as the most attractive or most popular. Then a friend suddenly has a change of circumstance and becomes the central focus of the group's admiration. Your ego takes a hit every time you see her. Her new success seems to take away what you had. You can't stand to see her enjoying the limelight and secretly relish the moments when you can take her down a notch with a comment here or there about things she's insecure about. Of course you could never confront her. The humiliation of admitting to feeling envious means there's not a chance in hell that you could be honest with her. So you find more subtle ways to numb the envy and regain some ground on that social scoreboard.

You draw close to the others in the group, exclude her when you can, and at the slightest hint of ill-feeling toward her from anyone in the group, you are ready and waiting to fuel that fire. These sorts of scenarios are often stoked with passive-aggressive communication. If it is being directed at you, then taking into account the full context of the insecurity fueling it can help you to feel it less personally and instead see it as their pattern of behavior that they are responsible for.

How to respond to it

So how are you supposed to deal with passive aggression? First and foremost, don't lose sight of you. Keep your own integrity, objectives, and values in full view at all times. Expect to feel a strong urge to give in to it as a way to avoid the uncomfortable feelings that come up. But remember that playing the game is not the only way to survive through this. In certain situations, when you have no power or means of escape, it is necessary to play the game until you are free to choose otherwise. But in most everyday situations, joining the power battle means you lose. Choosing whether to play the game is often a weighing up of risks and rewards. Among the greatest risks are the gradual corrosion of your own integrity as you lose sight of your own values and your vision of the sort of person you want to be. Some battles matter. Others are a waste of your time.[3]

When dealing with someone who has a tendency toward covert narcissism, any attempt to address the slight directly will often lead to an explosive argument that results in such a mess (and no resolution) that you regret ever trying to stand up for yourself. Or simple questioning about whether they were intending to be hurtful can be easily brushed off with an "I was

"Some battles matter. Others are a waste of your time."

joking! Lighten up" type of comment. Given that the passive aggression is likely to have resulted from a fear of confrontation, this will not open the door to a resolution.

It is possible to lean into the difficult conversation a little if you keep a tight hold on a non-blaming, transparent, respectfully assertive approach. While it is unlikely to lead to a miraculous apology on their part, simply letting them know that you sense they are not acting like themselves is a compassionate way to signal that you have seen their move but remain composed and unfazed, giving no fuel to their fire by acknowledging that they hurt you. Stay careful and stay clever in how you tread.

Resembling any kind of victim in your response to them renders them a winner in their eyes and runs the risk of perpetuating the behavior. It hands them the power to easily deny any such passive-aggressive intentions or mock your apparent overreaction and leave you feeling foolish.

Instead, stepping back from the game and watching them play it alone, grappling for power, is in fact winning. Just watch and learn, watch and learn. Do not indulge them or imagine that you can rescue them from their own poor choices of communication. You can't. Recognize your worthiness as a separate individual, whether they approve or not. Remember that you are deserving of good fortune as much as anyone else, whether they find it irritating or not. Even in the face of hurt, there is great power in choosing not to get sucked into such petty games that only serve to distract you from a better way of living.

In close relationships, getting some distance is sometimes necessary to help you keep your cool. But let your hurt and anger toward them for their betrayal be channeled in the direction that serves your agenda, not theirs. You have learned the painful way that this person does not fully have your best interests at heart, or at the least has poor communication skills. Take that learning and use the wisdom gained from this experience. To become whiny or complaining is a step down for you. Instead, step up, keep your composure, and do not adjust your standards to appease another.

Takeaways

- When you are on the receiving end of passive-aggressive behavior, take a step back and bring the wider power game into view. There is much to be learned from this experience, and this will not be the last time you encounter someone who uses indirect aggression to communicate.

- You can spot passive-aggressive behavior when someone's negative emotion is being expressed indirectly in a form of muted hostility, such as backhanded comments, sarcasm, or praise loaded with insults.

- Taking time to consider why someone is behaving this way toward you is a helpful part of the process in dealing with it because you're automatically left questioning if it's your own fault, when it's more likely to be reflective of their own patterns of relating to others.

- Don't lose sight of you. Keep your own integrity, objectives, and values in full view at all times. Remember that playing the game is not the only way to survive this. In most everyday situations, joining the power battle means you lose.

CHAPTER 7

When your parents got it wrong

Children begin by loving their parents; as they grow older they judge them; sometimes they forgive them.

—Oscar Wilde, *The Picture of Dorian Gray*

A letter from me to you

Everyone's parents got things wrong. But some got it a lot more wrong than others. Some children make a smooth transition into an adult relationship with their parents. For others, it can feel like a constant source of pain and confusion. For the majority of this relationship you have been the child, with no control or choice about how the relationship stands. But then that relationship transforms from a child-adult relationship to an adult-adult one.

But being an adult doesn't necessarily mean you can now have the relationship with your parents that you always wanted. The only thing you can truly control is what you bring to the relationship. With that comes huge responsibility, both to enforce your own boundaries to protect yourself and also to acknowledge the role you now play in a relationship that might not be healthy.

When we think about our relationship with our parents, the tendency is to slip back into our core template for that relationship. Me as the child focusing on what I need from my parents, grieving for what I needed but didn't get, and fantasizing about being able to change them.[1] Or maybe dreaming of the day that they finally see the damage they've been doing all this time and come around to the idea of doing things differently.

A heartbreaking but also liberating reality of this new adult-to-adult relationship is that we cannot force insight or change onto anyone but ourselves. The heartbreaking part is that we often have to accept that a parent is not capable of the kind of relationship we wished for. The liberating part is that we can manage the whole relationship around more realistic expectations of them so that we can protect ourselves from the pain of their own personal patterns and still maintain some sort of rapport.

But this is no easy thing to do. Most people get the idea of reconciliation mixed up with the idea of winning. If the other person could just see all the things they get wrong, we'd be okay. But our only path to a better relationship is to ask ourselves, What am I doing that contributes to keeping us stuck? Not an easy question to put to yourself. For some, it may be that a failure to put up healthy boundaries has led to resentment and contempt. For others, it may be a sense of entitlement that ignores the parents' own struggles. Everyone's situation is unique, but if you are brave enough to answer it honestly, then the answer to the next question becomes easier to find. In what small ways could you make this relationship better for both of you? And if you work on repairing this relationship, what would that mean for your life?

Real-time tools

The tasks ahead begin with getting clarity on whether the best outcome for this relationship is gaining more closeness or less. It is easy to say that if a relationship is abusive or harmful, then you should end it, but in reality those situations are rarely so clearcut. They are often confusing and filled with both good days and bad. In those cases, getting an outside perspective from someone you trust is valuable.

But when the aim to reconcile and improve the relationship is already set, here are some tools to help guide you on that path.

Working out what is possible

For many people, there is friction around whether to lean into that difficult conversation with a parent or not. Before diving into a conversation about all of your parents' apparent shortcomings, be clear in your own mind about what you hope to achieve. Age alone does not guarantee new wisdom or emotional maturity. Parents may have as little insight into the impact of their mistakes as they ever did. If that is the case, then any attempt to reconnect with your parents through such a conversation runs the risk of it being thrown back in your face with full force. It is an illusion to think that if they could just see where they went wrong, everything would be better. Instead, the focus with the most to give back is on ourselves.

If your aim is to reconcile differences and build a deeper relationship with your parents, a big hurdle is the tendency to get caught up in fantasies about what a parent-child relationship should be like. But for most parents, there is no conscious decision to disrupt the relationship with their children. They, too, may be acting out unhealthy but largely unconscious vicious cycles that started in their own childhood. And while you cannot change any of those things for them, you must bring realistic expectations about what kind of relationship they are capable of having.[2]

You will probably be aware of their patterns that play out. In fact, you can probably predict the disruption before it happens. You know when they are the heart and soul of the party or when you will get the cold shoulder or when they will throw a fit of rage. Whatever it is in your family, if it is predictable, spend time reflecting on those patterns. Plan how you intend to cope and respond to these challenges in a way that ensures some self-preservation but also doesn't join the circus and bring more destruction.

Reducing the expectations we have of our parents is letting go, in some sense, of the child's role. But it also helps to detach slightly from feeling hurt and fighting about it. It's a quiet sense of knowing that allows you to build a relationship around their shortcomings. If they are unreliable, don't rely on them for anything that matters to you. If they become passive-aggressive when you share your personal achievements, make careful decisions to share with someone else. You cannot expect of them what they have never been able to give you. There is liberation in deciding to stop trying and to settle for the kind of relationship they are capable of that also protects you from the pain of trying to make it more. That might not be the close bond you always dreamed of, but what you get in return is something you can sustain and freedom from the fight to change the unchangeable.

"Free yourself from the fight to change the unchangeable. The focus with the most to give back is on ourselves."

Avoid the drama

Do you step into the child role again as soon as you enter your parents' house? Or do you maintain all the maturity that you bring to your other adult relationships? And when it comes to ruptures in the relationship, do you take the role of victim, blaming them for everything? Or perhaps one parent victimizes the other, and you step in as the rescuer.[3]

Destructive interactions usually see each person stepping into one of three roles:

- **Victim:** This is not an actual victim, but playing this role means someone feels and acts like one. They might convince themselves that there is nothing they can do about the other person or the situation. They feel powerless, persecuted, and oppressed, and refuse to attempt change. While it is a miserable position to take, it enables the avoidance of responsibility for change with all the effort and discomfort that it entails.
- **Perpetrator:** This person either casts themselves or is cast by others as the villain of the story. They may come across as blaming, superior, and critical or controlling. If they are challenged about it, they might become defensive or switch into a victim role, relinquishing their responsibilities.
- **Rescuer:** Taking on the role of rescuer often involves swooping in to take care of things and feeling guilty otherwise. But when those efforts achieve little, the rescuer may become angry and switch to perpetrator.

If their rescuing was helpful, it only serves to reinforce the victim's position as powerless and keeps them stuck. The payoff for the rescuer is superficially feeling good for helping others but is often an avoidance of their own problems.

In any conflict, one person taking on any of these roles invites the others to take the other roles. But all the roles are dysfunctional and only serve to harm the situation as a whole. Even as individuals play the game of switching between roles to manipulate one another, no one is taking responsibility to find any kind of peaceful resolution or to reconnect in an honest way.

As ruptures play out in the family, see if you can notice which roles each person is slipping into, often without consciously realizing. If you notice that you tend to take on the victim role with your parents, one way to step out of that is to focus on what you want from this relationship or situation, rather than zooming in on all the problems you don't want. Make a conscious effort to take radical responsibility for each challenging situation and bravely take the steps necessary to move things in a more positive direction.

If you recognize that you have a tendency to step into that rescuer role and enable the victim to stay stuck, don't be tempted to switch to the perpetrator when you get frustrated. Try seeing the person in that victim role as capable, even if they don't see it in themselves just yet. Do not overreach by taking any choices or actions that they could do for themselves, however tempting it is. The person in that victim role may even encourage you to do things for them, but remember this only *feels* like helping. In reality it is enabling them to remain a victim.

If you can acknowledge the times you might slip into a perpe-trator role, try to consciously shift toward assertive rather than punishing, challenging but not controlling. Refuse to start actively blaming or behaving in any way superior. That only invites the other person to take on the victim role and keeps all of you stuck in this cycle.

Don't slip into the worst relationship habits

The negative communication patterns most associated with the destruction of romantic relationships will also have a devastating impact on your attempts to have uncomfortable conversations with your parents. So make yourself aware of them before each interaction and steer away from them at all costs.

- **Criticism:** Not the constructive kind that helps people to see a way forward, but the attacking kind that suggests they are a lost cause. "You have always been such a cold parent! Why don't you ever visit me?"
- **Contempt:** Belittling remarks, sarcastic comments, and insults, or merely dismissing their concerns. When contempt leaks into our communication, it may feel subtle to us, but it rarely fails to hurt and is more likely to put someone on the defensive than to make them ready to listen.
- **Defensiveness:** This can feel like an impulsive reaction to criticism but reflects attempts to slip into the victim role and not take on responsibility for ourselves or deal with the interaction in a mature way.
- **Stonewalling:** At the end of the family get-together, you drive away bubbling with rage and let three months go by

before speaking to your parents again. Until the next time, when a similar situation occurs because nothing was resolved while you were stonewalling them.

Write a no-send letter

This is something that is often done in therapy. It is one way to get clarity on relationships that are confusing and layered with conflicting memories and interactions. If you know that your parent will never be capable or willing to listen and talk with the aim of resolving things, or if it seems impossible to speak without interruption or a fight, then this can be an interesting exercise to help work out what you can let go of and how you want the relationship to go forward, even without that person to collaborate with.

 Try this: Write a letter to the parent in question. Given that you never intend to send this letter, it doesn't matter too much about the order of things or how you say them. Just use this as an expression of all the things you would like to say and would like to ask them. Write down the patterns of harmful behavior, the effect of them, and how you intend to break those patterns going forward.

Write down how you feel about this parent and the relationship you are going to take responsibility for having with them from now on. The letter can include an offloading of all the most hurtful things they did, the special moments they ruined, the betrayals or abandonments, the cruel words. But also take time to explore the things they did for you that you feel grateful for, to recognize how they might have exceeded the standards of their own upbringing.

Remember, this letter is never to be sent. It is for you and your own clarity of mind so that you can act with informed and carefully thought-out intention.

Takeaways

- For a significant period you were a child with no choice or control over the relationship with your parents. While the tendency might be to slip back into the child role around your parents, this relationship is now adult-to-adult. You can now take responsibility for the quality of this relationship as much as they can.

- A painful realization is that our parents are sometimes unable to offer the kind of relationship we wish for. They come from their own complex childhoods, and it's possible they face barriers you cannot see. Setting realistic expectations for your relationship will lead to less hurt than trying to change someone.

- Many of us carry into adulthood the tendency to still view our parents as having responsibility for the quality of our relationship with them. But, once in adulthood, we can ask ourselves, how am I contributing to keeping this relationship stuck? What small things could I change to make this relationship better for both of us?

- It is not our fault that we had the early years that we did. But it is now our responsibility to do what we can to heal and to break the cycles so that we can have healthy relationships and parent our own children in the way that we aim to.[4]

- Make use of some of the best relationship advice on how to deal with conflict. Holding back on contempt, criticism, defensiveness, and stonewalling could make a significant difference to how effectively you communicate.

- Now that you are no longer a defenseless child but a responsible adult in this situation, don't be tempted to slip into the role of victim, perpetrator, or rescuer when disagreement arises. By doing so, you invite others to take on the corresponding roles and block the path to true reconciliation.

CHAPTER 8

When you get it wrong as a parent

There was no way to be a perfect mother and a million ways to be a good one.

—Jill Churchill

A letter from me to you

If you were knocking on my door right now, I'd hand you a cup of tea and sit you down for a breather. Imagine if there was time for such a thing in the toughest parenting moments. Wouldn't it all go so much smoother?

Oh, the guilt and the shame that fills every cell in the body when we tell ourselves we just got it wrong. The physical pain that comes from thinking to yourself, *This is not how I want to be doing things.* Then the self-loathing takes over, and we go on the attack. *I'm such a bad parent. Every other parent can handle this. There must be something about me that makes this so hard. If I was getting it right, my child wouldn't be this challenging.* And so it goes on.

But let me ask a few slightly radical questions. What if you are not a bad parent? What if you're this human being who has spent several years ignoring your own basic needs in order to give everything you could to your loved ones? What if keeping up with the world's expectations of you seems to leave no room for you? And what if those unmet needs leave you inadequately fueled to give your best to the biggest challenge of your life? What if you're running on empty but expecting perfect performance without exception? Who else would you ever treat this way?

There is a never-ending stream of parenting bibles that claim to know how we should all be raising our children. The general gist has been to embrace, accept, and validate all of your child's emotions, whenever they make an appearance, with little mention of how you do that when you can barely contain your own. How on earth are you supposed to continue with that approach when your child has triggered shame, embarrassment, and rage, often in some sort of very public and humiliating experience. Many mothers today berate themselves for expressing any of those apparently unacceptable emotions in front of their children.

But I can't help but wonder, what are we really teaching our children about those emotions if we see them as unacceptable in ourselves? Perhaps allowing yourself to be as human as you allow your kids to be means acknowledging how we feel and doing what we need to do in order to express it and calm down again without doing anything we regret. Or when we do make mistakes in anger, being the adult, remembering what matters most, and initiating repair of the connection between you.[1]

If you have been driving yourself into the ground trying to do your best for your family and still you are plagued by feeling like it's not enough, I see you, my friend. I see all those layers of frustration pushed down like sediment. I see all those ways you take care of things that go unnoticed. I see all those times you are doing such a great job and not giving yourself credit for it. All of those things show you that, however you might have gotten it wrong today, you have the most important thing intact. You love your child more than you can articulate. And so, after you rest here for a moment, you will recalibrate, stand up, and reconnect with those little people who mean the most to you in the world. And you may not see right away how much good that does, but I'll bet it's more than the damage you thought you had done.

Real-time tools

Nothing brings up intense emotion quite like parenting. It is par for the course. But you can guarantee that when we do something we regret and deviate from how we want to parent, it has something to do with big emotions that caused us to lose sight of that for a while. Therefore, rather than ruminating over the apparent psychological damage you imagine you've caused your child, that time would be better spent attending to your own emotion state for a moment so that you can return to the job of parenting with the frame of mind that is necessary to do the job well.

Take a minute—parents have feelings too

Bringing our best to any situation can be done only when we take a moment to actively choose the demeanor and mindset that will make it possible. Dr. Becky Kennedy, a clinical psychologist, makes it clear that you don't have to be emotionless to parent well.[2] But what you must do is listen to what those emotions tell you about your own unmet needs. You then have to commit to meeting those needs that prevented you from parenting in the way you want to. And you must repair the relationship when you do make mistakes. No need to carry any illusion that a perfect parent never gets frustrated or angry or does anything wrong. In fact, I would argue that it is more beneficial for everyone involved if you have a human moment, then take responsibility as the adult to repair and to help yourself do things a little differently next time. Here is a recap on this:

1. Turn to your own emotion, not with judgment but with curiosity. Ask yourself: What does this tell me about what I need?
2. Whether it was tiredness, lack of sleep, lack of social contact, or overwork, commit to addressing the contributing factors as much as you can. It might be a small change like an early night to bed, or it might be something bigger. Meeting your needs in whatever ways you can is going to improve life for the whole family.
3. Repair the relationship with your child. Be clear about how you want to do things differently and that you are working on it. This doesn't have to erode boundaries and rules. For example, you may have upheld a necessary boundary but lost your temper in the process. So your repair might acknowledge that you didn't mean to shout.

Regulate by giving yourself what you give to everyone else

If you tend to go into a downward spiral of self-recrimination after a parenting mistake, this next exercise can help to stop that destructive thought process in its tracks, bring down the intensity of emotion, and enable you to get back in the game.

 Try this: Place your palm over your chest and hold it there for a moment.

Allow your breathing to slow, back to its natural rhythm.

And feel the warmth of your hand radiate on your chest.

Allow everything to slow.

Then say these words to yourself, either out loud or in the quiet of your own mind:

- This is tough.
- I am trying my best with what I have right now.
- It feels so painful when I get it wrong because I care so deeply.
- It is love that enables me to steer back in the direction I want to go after I fall.

Allow yourself to sit, breathe slowly, and repeat any of these words that might have resonated for you, or find your own, until you feel able to return to the challenge you're facing. These moments of recentering can be small: a deep breath and a few words to yourself in the most challenging of scenarios that shifts the focus of your attention and clarifies in your mind how you intend to approach this. Alternatively, recentering can be used as a part of longer meditations that can aid in accessing a form of self-compassion. For those who would like to use longer guided meditations, these can be found for free on my YouTube channel (@DrJulie).[3]

The balancing act

The friction felt daily by every parent is the tension between try-ing to equip your child for real life with all its demands, bound-aries, and structure, while patiently connecting with them in a way that feels like unconditional love and belonging. The speed and complexity of modern life often feels in direct conflict with the fundamental need for children to take their time and feel con-nected to parents. But rather than opposites in battle, perhaps they are two paths that run parallel. You cannot have both feet on one path without shifting from the other. Often as parents we feel like we ping-pong back and forth. But we aim to have one foot on the "connection" path and one foot on the "meet life's demands" path. How liberating to realize that you cannot be fully immersed in both of those at the same time, almost like walking a balance beam. There probably is a sweet spot somewhere in the middle, but as you move along at pace, the most effective way to balance is to pay attention to when things are weighted too much toward one side and put conscious effort into shifting the other way. It's a constant process of paying attention and shifting direction. When you are focused on rebalancing, there is no time for condemning yourself for needing to rebalance. It's simply the process. You can't expect yourself to stay in that sweet spot for too long when you're moving forward at the same time. Moments of disconnection are inevitable. Minimizing the impact comes from zooming in on re-pairing that rupture.

Deciding whether to apologize

This is often a difficult thing to acknowledge, but parents don't always feel positively toward their children. At times when they persistently behave in ways that we find detestable, we may even feel dislike toward them. The shame that can follow prevents us from even being able to acknowledge it, let alone apologize for any mistakes we made. The urge is to carry on as if nothing happened, our own defenses preventing us from repairing and reconnecting. Instead, we can feel a widening void between us, a distance that makes reconnection feel ever more difficult.

Many people are also apprehensive about apologizing to children for fear of sacrificing some of their authority or giving the impression that the inappropriate behavior is permissible. But not talking openly about both your child's behavior and your own, and being unable to model healthy apologies without trampling over important boundaries, serves to perpetuate the buildup of resentment in parenting. We cycle from guilt to anger and back again, treating nurture and structure as opposing forces.

We are the first generation to be exposed to the idea of modeling healthy apologies to children, and few, if any of us, were parented in that way. Our parents and their parents before them were generally taught to brush shameful acts under the carpet. If you don't mention it, it goes away. Generations of children have not had the chance to witness their grown-ups repairing ruptures in their relationships. But, imagine for a moment, one of your own parents coming to you and acknowledging the pain you must have felt from something they did, even if it occurred years ago.[4] How would that feel? And, even all these years later, would your relationship benefit from that? Human relationships gain something fundamental from repair: a trusting connection that can often be more powerful than the initial rupture.

No one ever taught us this. We are the first generation to be fed this idea that we should do anything other than get children to follow the rules. We are attempting to parent this way without the benefits of having been parented in this way. But, if you recognize this to be something that could aid in the repair and reconnection with your child, then it's worth a try.

Shifting state

So what does repair look like and when do we need it?

It's tremendously difficult to even contemplate repairing and reconnecting when you feel anger, rage, frustration, embarrassment, or shame. This is why looking after yourself in that moment must be a part of the equation. I would say this is the most important part of the process, because only when you are in a high-emotion, high-stress state do you say or do things to your children that you later regret. Taking one deep breath and going back in to try again is not giving yourself enough of a chance.

There are different ways to shift your emotional state in the moment. Moving the body is one way, changing your physical location is another. Spend a few moments outside to breathe or be in nature. There's a shift in perspective that can come from looking up at the stars or talking briefly with a supportive loved one. These simple things can make a huge difference in allowing us to reflect and refocus on how we want to connect with our child while also guiding them in a way that makes us proud. Don't neglect this step; without it, the rest is less likely to succeed.

The sooner we can bring down the anger we feel toward them and ourselves, the sooner we can reconnect with them.

"Moments of disconnection are inevitable. Human relationships gain something fundamental from repair."

Meet my own needs? Dream on.

This is something to think about once the rupture has passed and you notice that your reactions may have something to do with some of your own unmet needs. But how do you work out what your needs are? And how do you meet them when you're invested in being the most selfless parent you can be? Start with the essentials. Am I hungry? Am I tired? Am I lonely? Am I stressed? And when the answers to your questions are yes, don't be tempted to shrug them off as just another part of parenting. Many people are living under immense pressure as they juggle parenting with keeping a roof over everyone's heads. But if there is any possible way that you can better meet your own needs in this equation, it will benefit the whole family.

One common thing we feel guilty for as parents is when we burst at the seams and big feelings seem to come out of nowhere: a small spill that leaves you weeping on the kitchen floor. These moments are not who you are. They are signals, shouting at you to put something back in the tank because you're running on empty.

Many people who have established a lifetime habit of parking their own needs to put everyone else first find the reality of looking after themselves tremendously difficult. Doing these things is not difficult, but feeling the guilt that comes with it is uncomfortable at best, unbearable at worst. Your inner monologue won't stop telling you that this is a waste of time and unforgivably selfish. But we underestimate the ripple effect of doing things that enable us to bring our best selves to our loved ones.

If you tell yourself that all of your mistakes will cause long-lasting damage, then you must also acknowledge that everything you do to improve your chances of not making those mistakes also brings long-lasting positives to your whole family. Weakening yourself to strengthen others is not the optimal outcome if there is any way that the whole family can thrive.

What are you going to put in place today to start meeting one of those needs? Because despite being a parent, your basic human needs are still essential, and you cannot be the parent you aim to be without meeting those first.

Takeaways

- Experiencing anger and frustration does not make anyone a bad parent. Use them as signals to check in with your own needs.

- Take whatever time is available to you and give the emotion the time and space to pass naturally, or at the very least, to find some self-compassion and refocus on how you intend to approach this.

- If you have had time to calm the body and recalibrate, you are in a much better position to approach the situation in the way that you want to.

- Repairing any rupture in your relationship allows you both to reconnect and to move on.

- Meeting life's demands and having a nurturing connection with your child often feel like opposing forces. But it is okay to shift between the two as long as you don't spend all of your time in just one of those camps.

CHAPTER 9

When they don't love you back

Love is not love,
Which alters when it alteration finds.

—William Shakespeare, "Sonnet 116"

A letter from me to you

When the person you love doesn't love you back, or when they actively try to hurt you, the shattering seems to ripple out and touch every part of you. Every vision you had for a future together, every adjustment you made to live alongside them, every thread of confidence you had. At this point we can lose sight of the fundamental truths that could have helped us move forward through the darkness. So this letter is a reminder of a few of those truths.

The only way through the pain of a broken heart is to find ways to move forward so that you can witness yourself doing just that. You cannot sit in the darkness and convince yourself that all will be okay, you have to make it okay. The belief that you can have a future beyond this point comes when you prove it to yourself.

Nothing can trigger our most painful core beliefs about not being enough quite as much as the person you love not loving you back. You indulge the fantasy that if you could just be better, that person would love you. This goes beyond the more helpful self-reflection on how you may be able to do better in relationships in the future and dives into the deep end of self-loathing. The voice of shame that says you are doomed to be rejected because of who you are. What we miss while stuck in this rumination is the understanding that our worthiness need never be on the line. Our inherent worth as a human being stands separate from the actions of others. So their affections are not a measure of us. They never were. Let your response to this and the fight to start a new chapter be the measure of you instead.

If you notice this kind of inner questioning about whether you were ever deserving of the relationship, do not indulge it. Do not spend your time trying to answer that, for it is the wrong question. Instead, recognize those doubts as an indication that this was not the person for you. A relationship you do not feel deserving of is not one you could ever feel safe in.

Another trap that will keep you stuck in the darkness of heartbreak is the idealizing or villainizing of the person who did not love you back. When you idealize them, you recall only the most desirable aspects of their character and remember only the fondest of memories. You immerse yourself in the good and mute the memories of their mistakes and the ways they disappointed you or hurt you. Or you villainize them and sentence yourself to living in anger and bitter resentment of all the bad they did to you. When we are not in the pain of heartbreak, it is much easier to understand the true complexity of each individual without branding anyone as simply good or bad. Doing so only keeps us trapped in idolizing someone who, by virtue of their rejection, could never have been perfect for us, or in villainizing, keeps us locked in a victim role and a life that is plagued by bitterness and resentment rather than fighting for a new future of our own creation.

Healing and moving on is not the same as forgetting. Turning your attention from this person doesn't mean you have to stop yourself from thinking of them. Of course, they will come to mind in every spare moment while you are grieving. While they might remain a part of the story so far, moving on simply means filling the space they left in your life with other connections, contributions, and endeavors that add to your life in a meaningful way.

Real-time tools

It is no exaggeration to say that one grieves when a relationship ends. The natural grieving process is a response to loss, even if the person lost is still living. You might stop sleeping, lose appetite, find it generally difficult to function. It is not unusual to see classic symptoms of depression for a while. If the person was a big part of your life, it also isn't surprising that your sense of identity and belonging is ruptured. So, for a time, you feel adrift and confused about your place in the world and what the future holds for you. It is quite possible that many of your ideas for the future included this person and were influenced by their own dreams and ambitions.

Now all those shared visions and shared responsibilities are exclusively yours. That is both liberating and terrifying. It cannot all be worked out at once. With all big tasks, the only real way through is with the patience to take one step at a time and to not simply wait for recovery and healing but to use everything at your disposal to fight for it. The psychologist Guy Winch says to identify each of these voids and fill them.[1] Whether it be lost social circles, activities you once enjoyed together, or plans for the future, each of them can and must be rebuilt so that you can reestablish a solid foundation for your life and how you see yourself within it.

Doing this helps you to recognize that your lost person was just one piece of the puzzle—not the whole thing.[2] While you will feel the urge to withdraw from the other layers of your life, it is wholly necessary to hold on to these tightly and to continue to nurture all the other parts of your life that make it worthwhile and meaningful. As a friend, sibling, parent, colleague, teacher, or student, there will be many responsibilities and people who depend on the value that you bring to their lives. They must absorb your attention for now. Once the relationship is over, you must invest your energy in things that help you move on.

Limit the rumination

When you find yourself asking why over and over, step back and acknowledge that yearning for a reason and an understanding is a normal part of the grieving process—but one that can keep you stuck if you give it too much of your focus. Much of the time this question is unanswerable. There is certainly no answer that is going to make it all feel easier or less painful. Your task right now is to take on this new reality and find a way to move forward through it.

Nurture the relationship that continues

The relationship that continues is of course the one with yourself. It is hard not to slip into the blame game and torture yourself with fantasies about what you could have or should have done or not done, or what a terrible person you must be. Sitting in your own shame does nothing to help you. Even if you wish to pick apart the things you got wrong with the aim of breaking cycles and doing things better in future relationships, that learning can be effective only if you bring compassion to the shame minefield.

Extend that compassion into the other areas of your life because you are going to need it for a while, especially where there have been life-altering changes involved, such as moving, navigating co-parenting, or recovering from betrayal.

See through your own bias

When you notice yourself idolizing or villainizing the other person, call that out to yourself. Both are tempting, but both are biased and unhelpful. Hold those thoughts lightly with compassion for your need to feel some relief, but consciously place under the spotlight the reality that individuals are complex and rarely are either all good or all bad. If you find yourself constantly looking back with rose-tinted vision, it can help to simply keep a list of the ways in which that person was not right for you or made having a healthy relationship difficult. Remind yourself that missing someone does not mean they were right for you. Conversely, if you find yourself demonizing the person and subsequently living in anger and bitterness, you can create a list of their better qualities and acknowledge that they are not all bad.

"Missing someone does not mean they were right for you."

Takeaways

- When a relationship ends, a grieving response is natural, so allow space for this. You might stop sleeping, lose appetite, and find it generally difficult to function.

- Step into the other layers of your life that matter to you and focus your energy on things that help you recover your life and move on.

- Torturing yourself with blame for all the ways in which you weren't "enough" does nothing for you. If you wish to acknowledge your mistakes in order to break cycles for future relationships, that learning can take place only in compassion.

- Making a caricature of the two of you in your mind as victim, villain, or idol is a sign of a biased and inaccurate recall of events and will be largely unhelpful to you as you try to move on, leading either to resentment and bitterness or to the temptation to return to a relationship that was not right for you.

CHAPTER 10

When they love you but you won't let them get close

You can practice any virtue erratically, but nothing consistently without courage.

—Maya Angelou

A letter from me to you

It's deeply painful to feel detached from the people in your life, even more so when you realize that the hand pushing them away is your own. It's a feeling that you're somehow not a part of things, that you're always on the periphery of the group. You keep yourself close enough to feel some connection but with enough distance to feel safe. You still yearn for that connection just like every other human, but you never allow yourself to be fully at the center of things. But, while it is a choice to sit on the fringes, it's not necessarily a conscious one.

In fact, for some of us, satisfying that most basic human need for connection feels almost intolerable, and there is such visceral relief that comes from keeping interactions short and superficial. What appears to be a love for solitude turns out to be a kind of covert stress avoidance. And when you've been keeping your distance for a lifetime, it's hard to know how to be close to others. We may not have in our mind the template for relationships that would have otherwise been set in childhood, so interactions are filled with uncomfortable feelings that we may not even recognize. The not knowing and the constant self-doubt about whether we're getting it right and whether we belong here can make relationships feel more draining than fulfilling. It feels easier to keep just enough distance to take out the risk of rejection. After all, they can't hurt you if they don't really know you.

But, for all the risks we take when we invest in relationships, it turns out that life is much harder without them. If we don't open up and fully absorb the people we love into the pores of our lives, that space fills with me, me, me. We become increasingly preoccupied with the self. Constantly self-evaluating and attempting to become, in some way, a perfect person before allowing anyone else to come too close. Such a plan is quite enticing because it sounds like a safe path toward relationships. But in reality it takes you further and further from the deep connections that make life meaningful.

Those urges to keep people at arm's length don't indicate that anything is wrong with you. There was undoubtedly a time in your life when doing just that probably made sense for you.[1] But those echoes of the past are now outdated. Today, you don't need the safety of isolation. Today, you need people. Today, you need to love and be loved, to know and be known. When you start showing up for people in small ways that in the past you would have held back from, you will start to build some momentum in what will become the adventure of your life, and you will build relationships that, one day, you would not trade for anything.

Real-time tools

If you have read this far, you likely already recognize that the urge to isolate is detrimental to your life. You may have started to wonder if there is more to life than straining to endure the loneliness and emptiness that comes with keeping everyone at arm's length. But when you are trying to shift what might have essentially been a way of living since your very first relationships, where do you begin?

Don't let damaging beliefs take the driver's seat

One way that our early experiences affect our adult relationships is in what we learned about trust. If you live through certain life experiences that leave you carrying the expectation of being criticized, shamed, dismissed, ignored, hurt, or rejected, then why would you ever be in a rush to take down the walls that are doing a great job at protecting you from those things? It feels almost alien to initiate any kind of friendship or relationship, and when someone shows an interest in getting to know you, a voice is always there in the back of your mind suggesting that there must be an ulterior motive. Even if you override that narrative, it continues with predictions that, once they get to know the real you, their feelings will change. Why? Because, in your mind, there is something fundamentally flawed about you. You're just different.

"For all the risks we take when we invest in relationships, it turns out that life is much harder without them."

But we don't think about that too much. It's painful. Instead, we convince ourselves we're just highly independent and prefer our own company. While that can be true, it can also be code for: getting too close to people is highly uncomfortable, and being alone feels easier.

Feeling fundamentally flawed is often seen in those who experienced emotional neglect in childhood.[2] It is less about what happened to you and more about what didn't happen. Fundamental needs for safe, secure, responsive attachment that might not have been met. A child can grow up wondering, "What is wrong with me?," and their assumption that the problem is within them persists into adulthood.

There is no overnight cure to feeling fatally flawed. But recognizing how it shows up in adult life and acknowledging that it was created through a less-than-ideal environment, rather than reflecting reality today, is a huge step toward being able to take the wheel so that your fears of being deeply known by others do not drive you into isolation and loneliness.

Understanding attachment style

Adult attachment styles describe the way we manage intimacy and closeness in relationships, and reflect the main patterns seen in childhood. The attachment style we develop is the result of many factors coming together, including the maternal conditions you were born into, such as whether your mother was under significant stress or suffering from depression, whether she had social support, the quality of your parents' relationship, your own temperament as a newborn, and how much time you spent away from your parents. But research also shows that attachment styles are not set in stone. Our romantic relationships in adulthood continue to affect our attachment style for better or worse. Anyone with a secure attachment style can become more anxious or avoidant in their relationships after a negative experience. But the good news here is that things can also go in the other direction. If you recognize your own avoidant attachment style, then with time and effort this can be positively impacted by the powerful effects of being in a relationship with someone who has a more secure attachment style.[3]

Everything we have been describing so far—the avoidance of intimacy and closeness, wanting to be close to others but not feeling comfortable to do so, keeping your emotional distance— reflects an avoidant attachment style.

An avoidant attachment style is not a mental illness; it is a set of residual urges and behavior patterns that we have learned in order to manage the relationships we've had so far. Whatever the circumstances that contributed to this avoidant style, it is not a reason to become self-critical. The learning of those patterns was helpful in the situation when they arose, but it holds you back now.

While there is great potential to create life-altering change, there is no switch that instantly turns an avoidant attachment style into a secure one. A lifetime of learned patterns does not vanish overnight. Doing things the old way always remains an option, and at times a very appealing one too. But carving a new path means holding clear in your mind where that old path takes you and why this new path, still wild and fraught with situations that terrify you, leads to more deeply fulfilling relationships.

The very first step in developing a more secure pattern of attachment in your relationship is to recognize the patterns of your attachment style and to build a picture of how you might do things differently in a more secure relationship. It helps to build a clear picture of what you want instead, and why. Then we can move on to the how.

A plan of action is needed for learning to recognize both the emotional discomfort and the subsequent urges to pull back and how you intend to respond to them in a way that leads you toward people, not away. When you can calm the emotional response that comes up in reaction to closeness, the strong urges to isolate will calm too. Experimenting with new, less destructive ways to feel calm and safe are a key part of the process.

A great deal of the work will be in learning to pick up on attempts at connection from your partner, setting yourself a rule to respond to them, and having a plan for how you will do that, so that nothing is left to impulses that echo from the past. All very easy to say and very hard to do. That's why using professional help is worthwhile if you have access to it. For those who don't, journaling and writing is an incredibly helpful way to learn from each experience, to plan to respond rather than react, and to stay on track when you feel like giving up.[4] For a guide on using writing to help yourself through this self-directed change, a great place to start is the book *Opening Up by Writing It Down* by James Pennebaker and Joshua Smyth.[5] Whichever route you take, keep in mind that we are all a work in progress.

Trust starts with you

While it would make sense to expect a focus on how you interact with others, learning to trust must begin with the relationship to oneself. To build the courage to start trusting in others, we must trust in ourselves.[6] To trust in oneself demands a radical commitment to have one's own interests at heart, to do what's necessary to pick oneself up and nurture the self, and never to question one's own worthiness of love and belonging, even in the face of potential rejection, humiliation, or abandonment. These are the monsters under the bed of every close connection. What if they don't like me? What if they don't love me back? What if I allow myself to be seen, and they don't like what they see? What if I am exposed and humiliated for all of my inadequacies? What if my worst fears of not being enough come true? The only way to answer each of these questions is to know, without doubt, that you will be a constant source of love and devotion for yourself. When you know you can survive all of the above, you are free to risk all of it in the name of meaningful connection and deep, intimate relationships. It doesn't mean that leaning into uncomfortable conversations and excruciating intimacy is not difficult. But it lessens the risk from the complete disintegration of your sense of self-worth, to a painful learning experience that can be recovered from.

Spot the traps

Someone with an avoidant attachment style isn't necessarily a lone wolf. The need for attachment doesn't disappear, so you probably find yourself wrestling with that powerful attachment system, trying to suppress the urges to connect with the person you love to avoid the discomfort that comes up when you do. But the ways we keep loved ones at a distance are not always obvious. Here are some of those ways to look out for:

- Telling yourself that you're just independent and not the commitment type.
- Starting relationships with unavailable people, for example someone who is already in a relationship.
- Shutting down when things start going well enough for the other person to want to get closer and more committed to you.
- Magnifying all of the small ways that your partner irritates or annoys you rather than seeing the overall picture that includes many things to be appreciative about.
- Tending to miss signs of emotional changes in your partner or not treating them as a reason to connect with your partner.
- At times when you are disengaged from your partner and feel lonely, you might notice that you fantasize about ex-partners, despite knowing that those relationships were not right for you.

Keep a lookout for behavior patterns like these and notice how they highlight that avoidance of closeness and connection. Spotting those patterns is a major step toward being able to go against those urges and do something different.[7] For example, when you notice yourself becoming overly irritated by the small things your partner does, it is possible to make a concerted effort to seek gratitude and refocus on all the things you feel deeply thankful for in this person.

Mimic the secure partner

Simply trying to stop doing what comes most naturally is not a great strategy. It helps to have a clear vision of what you are aiming for if you are to stand any chance of hitting the target. You may have had relationships with secure partners in the past or present, in which case they can provide a good role model when you're trying to decide how to behave in various situations. Here are some of the features of a secure attachment style as they manifest in everyday life.

- Aiming to be responsive to a partner's needs and expecting the same in return. This means checking in with the other person occasionally and trying to offer comfort when they seem to need it, as well as communicating your own emotions and needs as clearly as possible.
- Treating a partner with extra-special care in a way that distinguishes them from everyone else and creates a protective bubble around the relationship. That might show up in small actions that communicate to a partner how special they are and how sacred the relationship is.
- In times of conflict, seeking to come together and resolve the disagreement and reconnect rather than avoid and leave things unsaid. This involves a willingness to compromise and an awareness that winning arguments does not create a healthy relationship.
- Resisting any urge to act defensively or to punish a partner during a disagreement. The key to this is in communicating one's own feelings clearly without attacking, and being willing to consider criticism from a partner and to make adjustments that could benefit the relationship as a whole.
- Refusing to play games during conflict. Resisting the temptation to slip into the roles of victim, perpetrator, or

rescuer that only look to win and don't serve the relationship as a whole.

The signature of all the differences between secure and avoidant attachment styles is the tendency of the secure to move toward closeness rather than away from it. This is not an easy shift to make for anyone who has an avoidant attachment style. So recognize the enormity of the task and take it in the smallest possible steps. Communicating to your partner about what you are working on and helping them to understand why you might naturally pull away at times will help them to get on board and encourage you while also showing some understanding during the moments when you might return to old habits.

Takeaways

- Urges to keep people at arm's length don't indicate that anything is wrong with you. There probably was a time in your life when doing just that made sense for you. When you realize that those patterns are now doing more damage than good in your life, there is the possibility of doing things differently.

- You can start to spot the often subtle ways that you avoid closeness and intimacy. Spotting those behaviors gives you the chance to make a conscious decision to change them. You can start showing up for people in small ways that in the past you would have held back from.

- If your tendency to keep people at arm's length is taking its toll on relationships that matter to you, then don't be tempted to justify that emotional distance by telling yourself you're just fiercely independent and not the commitment type. Working toward a relationship that more closely reflects a secure attachment is going to lead to happier and more fulfilling relationships.

- If you want to work on feeling more comfortable with intimacy, then sharing that goal with your partner is going to help them be more understanding when you pull away, and support you in the ways you find most helpful.

CHAPTER 11

When you want to win the argument

Judge your moves by their long-term effects on other people.

—Robert Greene, *The Concise 48 Laws of Power*

A letter from me to you

Whatever the other person has done or not done, in an argument we are usually fighting to get back the power and control or recognition and respect that we feel we have lost. And we all have a few moves up our sleeve that make us feel like we are doing that. But I'm guessing that most of your day-to-day conflicts are with the people who mean the most to you in the world. The people you chose to have in your life, and the people you want to keep there. The people who are on your team. Think very carefully before beating down your own team.

When you fight with the people you love, the only person who thinks you look good in victory is you. To those you defeat, the memory becomes less about how you turned out to be right than about how you made them feel crushed, unheard, and unloved. Their witness to how wicked you were willing to be in the name of winning an argument will corrode their trust in you for a long time to come.

If you are aiming to win arguments with the people in your life, pause for long enough to consider your future with them and the likely consequences of one of you feeling they have won and the other feeling they have lost. What are you really aiming for with this person? To prove yourself to be uncompromising and ruthless in getting your own way? These are not small questions. Winning every argument is not as satisfying and victorious as it may seem. It can lead to a very lonely existence in which all the things that truly mattered have been destroyed in pursuit of being right about all the things that turned out to matter a lot less.

But being able to see this bigger picture does not mean you must shy away from difficult conversations and simply appease others to keep the peace. That will do its own damage to the relationship. We all have to work through disagreements. But if we do so with the aim of resolution rather than victory, everything changes. Neither person needs to feel beaten down by the process. The outcome might not be perfect, and it might be a dispute that comes up several times before you find a resolution that works for both of you, but keeping your eye on the fact that you want this person to love and respect you in the future will help you to resist the temptation to bring them to their knees with an unrestricted verbal assault that scorches the earth between you and does lasting damage to your relationship.

Real-time tools

However appealing it can be to unleash your anger in the heat of the argument, pausing to engage fully with a few important questions is a quick and easy way to see past the fog of anger and prevent mistakes that could cost you deeply in the future.

The first thing to consider here is who are you fighting with and what are you fighting about? What is your future with this person? And of what consequence is winning or losing?

What do you want for this relationship in the long run? To end it? To improve it? To co-parent without making each other's lives a living hell? And when it comes to the issue of disagreement, how does that fit into that bigger picture? What are you trying to get across to this person, and what do you think they are trying to communicate back?

Be the first to listen

When emotions are running high, we often start preparing our comeback before the other person is even halfway through their sentence. Everyone wants to be heard. No one wants to listen.

At this point, anyone who is able to see through the emotional intensity to take on board the other person's perspective is more likely to make good progress. Pausing your own crusade to listen may feel like giving in but doesn't have to be.

When someone is being shouted at, criticized, accused, or judged, the shutters come down and they are instantly focused only on protecting themselves. People are most open to compromise when they themselves feel heard and understood. There is great power to bring an argument under control when we simply and calmly listen and then demonstrate that we've done so. This is not the same as saying they are right; it is saying, "I see you and I am willing to consider that your perspective on this differs from mine."

Signaling that you are not a threat with a deliberate change of tone and volume is a powerful way to de-escalate and create a calmer space in which you can both start listening to each other once again. Anything that nods to the fact that your relationship and life together stretches way beyond this small moment. All of these things can see an almost immediate effect in everyone lowering their weapons slightly and taking a breath.

Don't throw daggers

Hold tight in your mind that, in every argument, everyone thinks they are right, everyone thinks they have access to the absolute truth. But all we really have are two different versions of what "right" could be, depending on your perspective. The basis for coping with conflict between you and a loved one is basic acceptance of their personality.[1] Whatever you think of their behavior or the things they are getting wrong, if you want the relationship to thrive, the last thing you want to do is slip into showing contempt for their very character and attacking them based on that. Showing contempt for who they are as a person changes everything.

When the other person is the one losing control, it is easy to spot by the shift from logical argument to name-calling and personal attack. This happens when they have scraped the bottom of the barrel of their argument and have nothing left but to throw the damn barrel at you instead. Do not let this be your cue to do the same. You don't have to accept their characterization of you in this moment, and it's easier not to if you can spot the pattern and recognize that it is not personal. They feel their back up against the wall and are most probably acting out of fear or hurt. Whether you think you had anything to do with that or not, it helps everyone if you can see it and feel a degree of compassion for it. That way you are less likely to lose control and join the verbal brawl and they are less likely to escalate in theirs.

Strength in flexibility

The best kinds of fights involve compromise without giving up too much. There are ways you can be flexible without eroding your sense of self and the personal boundaries that keep your integrity and agency intact. The challenge here is that nobody plans to fight with their partner or loved ones. Disagreements pop up when we least expect them, and we don't get the chance to sit down and think through what we are willing to be flexible on and when it's important to hold firm. So there will be times you get this wrong. The key is to be willing to reflect on situations that don't go as you'd like, and consider what you need to do differently next time. If you notice that the other person is always the one to apologize and compromise, it might be your turn to work on being more flexible. If they breach personal boundaries and you notice your tendency to be railroaded into their latest agenda, then making a clear list of boundaries to start keeping is wise. It is easier in the light of day, after the storm of an argument, to think about the times you keep saying yes when you want or need to say no, or times when you know you are being too rigid. Getting a concrete idea of those will help you to spot them as soon as they come up in future arguments and increase your chances of choosing a different path next time.

Slow things down

When the time comes that you do need to stand up and assert your own boundaries or needs, there are two hurdles that can hold you back from doing this successfully. The first is immersing yourself too deeply in empathy for them that you disengage with your own self; the second is being intimidated by the intensity of their emotion. Anger and raised voices in others can set all the alarm bells off in your own mind and scramble your thoughts on the arguments that you need to hold firm to. When this happens, it helps to slow down the tempo so that impulse does not have the upper hand over carefully considered moves.

When the aim is to be heard, composure is your superpower. At best, anger distracts from the validity of your argument, making you appear less credible. At worst, your anger hurts the other person, and their defenses go up, leaving you with no chance of being heard. Communicating clearly involves stating what you know to be true with calm composure and confidence, even when your emotional hackles feel raised inside.

You could say anger is a last-resort emotion. Until you are out of options, anger is not going to optimize any careful route out of this disagreement. Going in too strong might cause the other person to back down. But do not mistake that appeasement for agreement. If you feel like you are close to losing control, state that clearly and leave the room to give yourself space to get calm before continuing.

"When the
aim is to
be heard,
composure
is your
superpower."

Don't be the judge and jury of their experience

In arguments, some people grant themselves a position of authority in determining when the other person's feelings are valid and when they are not. If you find yourself tempted to do that, pause. Telling someone they shouldn't feel something when they already feel it does nothing to help that feeling disappear. The more likely outcome is that you add in a dose of shame to go with it, promptly shutting down any possibility of having a reasonable conversation that might lead to reconnecting.

You don't have to agree with their perspective to acknowledge that, in their position, this is how they feel. Giving them space to feel whatever they feel is a key stepping-stone on the path to reconnection. This is yet another occasion when it helps to shift from judgment to curiosity. In the heat of an argument, we are steeped in judgment. We are on guard, protecting our own point of view as the one and only truth. Why bother trying to understand their point of view when I know mine is the right one? Well, if your goal is to maintain and build a relationship, it will be a healthy one only when both of you recognize that you are two separate individuals who will always see things and feel things from your own angle. Working to understand something is not the same as allowing yourself to be convinced by it. You are not giving in. Saying "I hear you" is not the same as saying "I agree." Allow their emotion to be present, knowing that you can reach an appreciation of it, without having to be convinced that it is the best way to see the situation.[2]

126

Spot your own biases to argue better

Confirmation bias is something to look out for in arguments where logic seems to have gone out the window. This is our normal human tendency to interpret information in a way that reconfirms our preexisting beliefs. No argument is ever purely about the here and now. If I hold core beliefs about not being good enough or I expect others to lose interest in me and not care about me, then all the scenarios that could possibly be interpreted in this way will be picked up by my radar as evidence that indeed this person does not really care and I am not good enough for them. Those points on the radar will light up in a way that evidence to the contrary won't. We do this even when our beliefs are harmful to us because our past experience has created our template for the world and can't easily be reshaped.

Emotional reasoning leads to destructive arguments. *I feel it, therefore it must be true. If I am offended or hurt, you must have done something wrong.* This overlaps all too comfortably with confirmation bias. *I have a deep underlying sense that I am not lovable, and when my partner is late for a date I feel hurt, as if he doesn't care for me. I feel unloved by him, therefore, he is clearly not loving me enough.* In this, there's no consideration of his perspective whatsoever. Something small can touch on a past wound because the brain is trying to make sense of things by bringing into the equation times when you felt something similar in the past. This person and relationship may be very different from the one that created that wound, but the returning emotion is used to create our new reality.

Egocentric thinking is another bias to spot in arguments. This is when we see our own perspective as fact and neglect the reality that others have different values, ideals, and perspectives. This leads us to apply all the rules that we live by to them, often without telling them. If I have rules about and give meaning to taking my shoes off when I enter someone's home, then the moment a friend strolls into my kitchen with their boots on I might feel offended, neglecting the fact that my friend does not hold the same views and had no concept of mine on the subject. This bias can disrupt connection, as the people around us walk on eggshells, aware that if they put a foot wrong, they will be punished.

Overgeneralizing is a bias that many people are familiar with because we do it to ourselves when we are not feeling so good. At the end of a productive day, you drop your dinner as it comes out of the oven and proceed to write off the entire day as a disaster. The impact on your own emotional state in that sort of scenario is clear. But when we bring it into arguments, the damage can be severe. It often sounds like "You *always* leave your cups lying around!" or "You *never* help me clear up!" Instead of addressing each individual situation, we group things together and make a sweeping generalization, disregarding all the times that they might have done the right thing. As a result, they instantly feel unappreciated and their efforts dismissed. Suddenly, your chances of getting your partner to jump at the chance to please you, even with something that demands relatively little effort, is out the window. They will come back with defensiveness, not cooperation. You will undoubtedly be faced with a list of all their efforts and contributions because from where they are standing, you haven't noticed or appreciated any of it. Ditching this approach can change the game.

Takeaways

- When you fight with the people you love, the only person who thinks you look good in victory is you. To those you defeated, the memory becomes less about how you turned out to be right than about how you made them feel crushed, unheard, and unloved.

- If you are aiming to win arguments with the people in your life, pause for long enough to consider your future with them and the consequences of one of you feeling they have won and the other feeling they have lost. What are you really aiming for with this person?

- Winning every argument is not as satisfying as it may seem. It can lead to the destruction of all that mattered for the sake of being right about all the things that turned out to matter a lot less.

- Prioritizing a relationship does not mean you must shy away from difficult conversations and simply appease the other person to keep the peace. That will do its own damage to the relationship. We all have to work through disagreements. But if we do so with the aim of resolution rather than victory, the whole thing changes.

- Whatever you think of someone's behavior or the things they are getting wrong, if you want the relationship to thrive, the last thing you want to do is slip into showing contempt for their very character and attacking them based on that.

- It helps to slow down the tempo of a disagreement so that impulse does not have the upper hand over carefully considered moves. When the aim is to be heard, composure is your superpower.

CHAPTER 12

When it's hard to ask for help

If you want to go fast, go alone. If you want to go far, go together.

—'African proverb

A letter from me to you

Of all the chapters in this book, a part of me wonders if this one will be used the most. If there is one thing that we humans need, it's each other. But knowing you need help is no match for the torment of asking for it. Most of the time it's not even the fear that family and friends and colleagues won't be able to help. It's the fear that they will. Then you have to accept their kindness. Allowing someone to contribute goes against that drive to need no one, depend on no one.[1] So then you'll wrap yourself up in this story that your problems are too big or too small to warrant help. And with that story you'll convince yourself that somehow the biggest priority is not being a burden.

Thank goodness our ancestors didn't buy into that same story.

If they had, none of us would be here. Not doing it alone was their greatest triumph and the key to survival. They helped others where they could and accepted help where they couldn't. We don't think less of them for that. We celebrate them for it. Don't equate doing it alone with strength. The power is in the group.

To choose not to seek help when you know that you could benefit from it is putting the brakes on your own life. It's deciding that everything you're aiming for is not worth devoting all the resources available to make it happen. It limits your learning and your growth. It makes you feel infinitely more alone. And it greatly increases your chances of giving up. If what you're aiming for is huge, then you need to be clear in your mind that no one who achieves great things does it alone. They all have help from different directions. And they all accept it as the best way to maximize their own performance and ensure success.

That inner voice telling you to hide away from others and go it alone is usually fear talking. It's the instinct to keep yourself safe from the judgment of other people. But if you follow that impulse, you pay a heavy price. You feel safe for now, but you stay stuck. And that stuckness lasts for much longer than that feeling of safety. You get to prevent those other people from seeing your vulnerability, but in doing so you prevent them from seeing you become the best you could be. So we trade a moment of feeling exposed and vulnerable for a lifetime of wondering if things could have been better if we'd just been brave enough to ask for help.

It's in our very nature as humans to help and be helped. Not only that, by accepting help now, you put yourself in a position to be able to pass on that kindness to someone else and to give back more than you took.

Real-time tools

A couple of these tools can help to overcome both the thought processes and the emotion that can stop us from seeking the help that we already recognize we need. And once you've decided to do the best by yourself and ask for help, I've included a couple of things to keep in mind as you move forward.

A feeling does not make a fact

Any time that your mood is low, you might notice the tendency to feel things strongly and then be led by those feelings as if they were fact. This emotional reasoning can prove a real trap when you know that you could benefit from help. Low mood gives rise to feelings of fear, isolation, inadequacy, and unworthiness. We then assume that I feel it, therefore it must be true. So you might start to believe that you are alone and that you do not deserve help. But those thoughts were not the best reflection of reality. They were a reflection of your mood and emotional state.

If you know in your rational mind that seeking help would make sense but you're holding yourself back with thoughts that fit your mood rather than reality, simply reminding yourself that emotional reasoning is a thought bias can help you get a bird's-eye view of the process and take some of the power out of it.

For example, if you feel unworthy of help and you believe in that feeling as if it were a fact, you will start to act as if it were true. Yet we both know that there are people who disagree, people who know you are more than worthy of help. I know because I'm one of them.

"Knowing you need help is no match for the torment of asking for it. Most of what you will learn in life comes from action rather than thinking."

There are plenty of reasons to go for it and plenty of reasons not to. But most of the reasons not to are based on avoiding short-term discomfort. And holding on to the reasons not to seek help is guaranteed to hold you back. When you notice a bit of emotional reasoning going on, see if you can counterbalance it with alternative perspectives. Then make a strong conscious choice to turn up the volume on the thoughts that will most help you move forward. Writing it down can be especially useful at slowing the whole process down, giving you some distance from the thoughts and keeping it constructive to prevent it turning into rumination. List all those thoughts that are holding you back and appear to be wrapped up in emotional reasoning. Then make sure that each one has at least one alternative perspective next to it that is more helpful to you.

Turn it around

It is very easy for someone on the outside to see you as worthy of help, but much harder to get that objectivity in our own view of ourselves. One way to do that is to spend a few moments answering the following questions.

 Try this: Take all the problems you are facing right now and imagine that it's not you who is facing them at all. Imagine the person in your life you would least want to have these problems. What would it feel like to know they were facing all this?

If this person you care about deeply was facing this, what help would you want to give? Knowing what you know about the situation, what help would you see as most pivotal?

But now, imagine that you cannot help them in this way because, well, you don't know what they are dealing with. They decided to struggle alone and not ask for help. They know that asking for help could lead to better days ahead, but they see all the same barriers that you see.

Notice how the idea of that scenario feels substantially more painful, knowing how eager you would be to help, if only they would let you in.

Notice how you judge the situation, whether you think any less of the person for the context they find themselves in, or whether you simply see another human being who could do with a helping hand.

Picture that loved one and ask yourself: Do you see them as worthy of help?

Knowing the situation well, what help would most benefit them?

What would you want them to have the strength to do?

If you could, how would you reassure them that the best thing would be to ask for help?

And, if you see that person as worthy of your help, then you owe yourself the chance to be helped in the same way.

Speed

Once you have decided that asking for help is something you must do, the first principle that helps is speed.[2] The more you can close the gap between decision and action, the more likely it is to happen. At this point the biggest barrier is you talking yourself out of it. So find the smallest, most manageable of steps toward it and start taking action as soon as you can. Whether you want to feel better, know better, or do better, the only way is to take action.

When you stop thinking and start doing, you instantly get the benefit of simply witnessing yourself in action. If you ask for help once, you now have evidence for the future that you can.

If your first attempt to ask for help doesn't go quite as planned, maybe you'll notice you were hinting at rather than being clear about what you needed, or maybe you asked someone who turned out not to be quite the right person. Whatever the learning, it's your gain. Now you have the knowledge that you can ask, and some valuable evidence that you can survive even less-than-perfect outcomes.

Most of what you will learn in life comes from action rather than thinking. Holding that idea front and center makes action so much more inviting, even when it is terrifying. Being stuck in your own head, ruminating on whether you can or should do the thing that you suspect could be best for you, is akin to standing still and staring at the space between you and what you want. Taking a step forward is the only way you get physically closer to it. The result is less important than the act itself because action leads to more action, which generates momentum.

Don't leave anything to chance

Anything that feels initially overwhelming is easier to tackle when we break it down into concrete steps. Make a conscious effort not to look too far ahead, just get clear on the task in front of you.

 Try this: Write down a list of the people you could approach for help, with the most approachable at the top.

Next, write down exactly what you need: a listening ear, distraction, practical support, or simply connection and friendship. Once you have that clear in your own mind, it's easier to be concrete in what you are asking for. You won't have to think on your feet too much and risk slipping into more avoidant strategies like dropping hints. People are just as poor at responding to hints as they are to full-blown mind reading, so clarity is your friend.

Seeking help makes you independent, not codependent

Do not be tempted to conflate the idea of seeking help with codependency or any such terms reserved for those who may be unable or unwilling to be self-sufficient.

Dependency within families and communities is natural and increases our chances of both surviving and thriving throughout our lifespan.[3] From a secure base of trusted loved ones and helpers, you will be more ready to stand up and commit to taking the actions necessary to move you forward.

It makes sense to seek advice from those who have experience, to seek practical help from those who are competent, and to seek a listening ear from those who will grant us the space to talk openly. If codependency is what you fear, then commit to not letting others carry the entire weight of the problem. Honor their support by taking courageous action in the direction you need to go. A part of that commitment is to be savvy enough to realize when you are scraping the bottom of the barrel of your own strengths and to be brave enough to allow your loved ones to play their part.

Takeaways

- Not seeking help when you need it is a trade-off: a moment of feeling exposed and vulnerable versus a lifetime of wondering if things could have been better if you'd just been brave enough to ask for help.

- To choose not to seek help when you know that you could benefit from it is deciding that everything you're aiming for is not worth putting in all the resources available to make it happen. That greatly increases your chances of giving up. No one achieves great things by themselves. They all have help from different directions. And they all accept it as the best way to ensure success.

- That inner voice telling you to hide away from others and go it alone is usually fear talking. It's the instinct to keep yourself safe. If you follow that impulse, you pay a heavy price. You feel safe for now, but you stay stuck. And that stuckness lasts for much longer than that feeling of safety.

- Feeling undeserving of help or feeling like a burden does not mean that you are. Such thoughts and feelings tend to reflect mood, not reality.

- If you would see any other human in your position as worthy of a helping hand, then you are too.

- Once you have decided to ask for help, act with speed. Your biggest barrier now is you talking yourself out of it.

- Hints don't work. Be clear and concrete about what you need. This takes the guessing games out of it and makes it easier for the person who wants to help.

2

When it's hard to be with yourself

CHAPTER 13

When your inner voice is your own worst critic

It is not the mountain we conquer, but ourselves.

—Sir Edmund Hillary

A letter from me to you

When was the last time you fell short of your own expectations? What did you do exactly? And what was the silent, verbal onslaught in your mind that followed? How was that failure described? As the definition of you? A prediction of who you are destined to become? Or as another lesson learned and something gained?

If you think battering yourself with self-criticism doesn't have a host of unwanted side effects, you're wrong. Persistent self-criticism is like living in a very small room (about the size of your head) with a bully twenty-four hours a day, seven days a week. Nobody comes out of that brimming with confidence. The result will be the opposite. I know this because a significant number of clients land in my therapy room after years of blindly accepting such scathing self-talk as the truth and acting accordingly.

Despite this, many of them hold on to their inner critic and defend it. The way one might defend an emotionally abusive partner who claims they only criticize you for your own good: that they are simply trying to protect you from humiliating yourself. And you willingly subjugate yourself to that because you've convinced yourself it's necessary. If you're not careful, that critical voice starts to convince you that it's safer not to try than to risk failing. Then it spreads from this situation to that, and to another, until you feel your life start to shrink from all the opportunities that you won't allow yourself to risk taking.

Or let's say you don't retreat. Perhaps you see that inner critic as your most helpful servant and the only possible source of drive. So you strive forward and overcompensate to meet the unrelenting demands it comes up with every day in a bid to squash the insecurities. But you and the people around you sense that you're trying too hard and seem somehow a little less than authentic. Even if they do fall for it and bring forth the praise you were dreaming would make you feel like enough, what you then feel is slightly fraudulent and all the more anxious to keep it up. So the critic must be allowed to continue. Because still, it appears to keep confirming that you are clearly not cut out for this and need a constant kick up the backside, without which you would surely dissolve into a sloth of a human with no get-up-and-go.

At this point in your life, you have probably already been told that if you want to go far, it's wise to spend time with people who genuinely want the best for you. And you undoubtedly can already recognize what makes a good friend. Someone who will celebrate your victories, hold you steady when you fall, and help you find a new way forward without attacking and criticizing you. It's one thing to step away from friends who don't have your back. But what if that person is in your own mind? When that internal narrative shows such contempt for you, it feels impossible to change, because surely those thoughts are you. If you see those thoughts as your own self, of your own choosing, you will feel powerless to choose a narrative that's different. So you just live in line with the first thoughts that show up. And long after you may have gotten rid of the people in your life who were pulling you down, you continue to do their work for them in the privacy of your own mind.

Notice that. The next time a thought comes up that is thorny and filled with contempt for yourself based on something you did and how you did it, notice whether it sounds like the voice of someone it is healthy for you to spend time with. If the answer is no, then the good news is that you get to choose. You can interrupt the flow of that story and start to frame a new one. Something that sounds like the voice of someone you could trust, who has your back, who wants the absolute best for you, who has seen how far you have come and feels immensely proud, who says what you need to hear instead of taking the opportunity to slap you in the face with their words.

The person who gave you this book (even if it was the part of you that desires better for yourself) wants you to start recognizing what they see in you. They want you to feel your innate worthiness and potential, to see yourself how they see you, as someone worth knowing, worth encouraging. Someone with a future, given the right set of ingredients. They see the goodness in you, and they know that if you can hold on to appreciation for yourself, the way they appreciate you, that you will go far. That person doesn't need your thanks. They need you to take that recognition and run with it. Make them proud. Make yourself proud. And you cannot do that while you're tearing yourself apart in your own mind all day long. So start treating yourself the way they know you deserve to be treated. Because your potential reaches further than the images you can conjure up in your mind just now, and the only thing that will prove that to you is your own action.

Real-time tools

If you're still of two minds about whether you want or are able to let go of your inner critic, despite knowing its negative effects on you, then I have the tools for you here. You see, you don't have to eliminate all self-evaluation in favor of overindulgent, gooey-sounding self-talk. You can allow self-criticism in a way that truly helps you rather than hinders. We all want to thrive in life, but anyone at the top of their field who hires someone to keep them on an upward trajectory hires a professional coach, not a high-school bully. And for good reason. One helps you bring your best. The other does the opposite. This section lists a few tools for how to make self-criticism constructive and not destructive.

If you have to criticize, make it useful

Not all criticism is helpful. But how do we go from the kind of self-criticism that brings you down and kicks you while you're there to the kind that amplifies your drive to try hard and get back up after setbacks?

If you have ever tried to teach a child something that takes a long time to master, you'll have noticed that when they make mistakes or fall short, there are certain ways you can communicate to them that will get them excited about trying again, and other ways that will lead them to think this is just not their thing, so they'd rather just give up. That same equation works in our own heads, at any age. There will be things you have given up or avoided starting altogether in response to the inner critic that says you're not cut out for it. And the payoff is that you feel safe from the possibility of failure. For example, I want to write this book, but an incessant stream of consciousness says who the hell am I to think I can do this? Humiliation could be just around the corner if I keep going. Resting my fingers on the keys is a vulnerable place to be. The self-criticism entices me to apparent safety by making any attempt at improvement seem futile and risky. But avoidance does less for my confidence than getting words on the page.

So how do you self-evaluate and keep yourself accountable without causing more harm than good?

Five things to remove from your self-talk

1. **Global attack.** This is when you leap from acknowledging one shortcoming or mistake to launching a comprehensive assault on your character and personality, treating this one event as fundamental to who you are as a person and your inherent worthiness, and feeling you have no redeeming qualities to speak of. We have a tendency to do this in the heat of the moment when we feel angry or frustrated, often saying things to ourselves that would be called bullying if they were coming from someone else.

2. **Overgeneralizing.** While the global attack focuses on your personal attributes and worthiness, overgeneralizing is distinct in its focus on what happens to you. You allow one event to overshadow every other, as if one negative event writes off all the positive ones that came before it and predicts negative outcomes for everything that comes in the future. You might notice yourself overgeneralizing when one thing goes wrong, and you write off the whole day as a disaster. Or a relationship ends, so you tell yourself that all relationships are a waste of time. This one is the perfect recipe for giving up on something and a classic expression of a fixed mindset. That means you perceive your abilities to be fixed from birth, rather than a growth mindset, which acknowledges the potential for improvement with effort. You might see yourself as someone who is good at math until you find yourself failing at something beyond your current ability. Then the fixed mindset concludes, "I am no good at this," and gives up.[1]

3. **A mental pile-on.** After one mistake or setback we get to work recalling every other failure we have ever been responsible for. Our inner world starts to sound like an online hate campaign that escalates way out of proportion to the original error. Thinking in this way understandably sends your emotion state and mood into a downward spiral, which is not conducive to learning from the experience or leaping back up to try again.

4. **Contemptuous language and name-calling.** When one person shows contempt for another in response to their shortcomings, the natural reaction is often to stop listening

and start defending. All progress and the chance for learning stops in its tracks. But what happens when we show such contempt toward ourselves? When the words in our own minds sound something like *I hate you! You are utterly useless!* In these moments, rather than defending, we accept such self-loathing as valid, and we start to behave and treat ourselves as if it were true.[2]

5. **Self-protection.** When faced with a verbal onslaught from someone, the impulse is either to fight back or to escape the situation. But when the attacker is us, the defense becomes subconscious. We impulsively give in to all the urges to seek safety and comfort. Maybe that is to avoid the thing we wanted to work on and tell ourselves that we didn't want it anyway. Or we start to blame others to relieve some of the weight of the shame that comes with the way we attacked the very core of our own character for this failure. Whatever the mechanism of self-protection, they all tend to lead us away from the insight that would support growth and improvement.

Five things to include in your self-talk instead

1. **Pick your perspective.** As I have already pointed out, coming at the truth from new angles will bring you slightly different experiences of that reality. When you are thinking about yourself, it is important to step back and get a bird's-eye view of the event in question. This allows it to be seen as just one location in a much bigger landscape. In some psychological

therapies we create a timeline of events on paper that can stretch the whole lifespan. It can be a great tool for taking events that seem overwhelming at the time and integrating them into the broader narrative of your life, shifting the perspective on it as you do. One event cannot define a multilayered, multidimensional person who contributes to the world in many different ways and aims to continue to learn and improve beyond every individual attempt, whether it be in victory or defeat. One perspective to always search for is any valuable and useful learning for your journey and ambitions that extend far beyond this one event or mistake. Seek out the lessons that you can use to strengthen your resolve in the face of similar situations in the future.

2. **Action-evaluation only.** Our natural human tendency is to evaluate our personality and intrinsic self-worth, both of which feel unchangeable and lead to shame rather than anything genuinely helpful. In the service of getting to where you want to go, turn what sounds like evaluation of your character into evaluation of your action. This means focusing on specific events, behaviors, and choices. It means being as clear and concrete as you can, in the same way you would for someone you were trying to coach toward performing at their best. No learning can take place while you are busy trying to grapple with your worthiness as a human being. When that is under threat, it will always take priority in your mind and lead to the impulse to self-protect. But when your intrinsic worthiness is not in question, you are safe to look at your mistakes and learn. So always keep that off the negotiation table. You cannot thrive without it. When there

is something you are doing that isn't working out for you, aim to keep a sense of agency in the solving of this problem. To do this, focus on the options available to you. If you fail a test and conclude it's because you are useless, there is nowhere to go with that except into a downward spiral. But when you keep your personality out of it and start looking for chances to retake the test and begin working on the parts you got wrong, then you will find energy for forward motion once again. When we can see options in front of us, then we don't stop to contemplate whether we should just give up and hate ourselves forever.

3. **Choose your words carefully.** Imagine a child in your life you deeply care about turns out to have an outstanding talent in their chosen sport, and you have the task of coaching them through the wins and the losses, the highs and the lows of striving with ambition. On their way to great things, they make some mistakes and suffer big defeats, and it is your job to be the first to speak to them and scoop their confidence off the floor. In these moments, if you truly wanted the best for this child, you would make a considerable effort to select your language with precision. The same goes for the way you respond to yourself among the triumphs and the setbacks. Your words have power, so treat them as such. How can you frame reality in a way that removes any unnecessary psychological threat and instead extends a hand to pull you back up ready to go again?

4. **Be honest.** Tossing out handfuls of empty positives like confetti at a wedding will fall just as lightly. Your words will have a strong impact on how you feel and behave only if you can trust them. So make it truthful every time. Many

people assume that the only two options are the "good vibes only," overindulgent, sugarcoated self-talk that sounds like lies, or the truth delivered as a verbal assault that leaves you curled up in a ball wishing you had never been born. But these are not the only options. We can go with straight-up honesty that is warm and genuinely wants to help you thrive. An honesty furnished with respect and a dose of curiosity for finding a chance to learn in everything.[3]

5. **Turn to face the world.** Sometimes the best remedy for constant self-attack and self-evaluation is to stop focusing on the self altogether. The more we think about ourselves, the more miserable we become.[4] We are social animals. We are supposed to be looking out for each other and working out how we can best contribute to the group effort. Today's world encourages self-obsession because it opens up a chasm of insecurity that can be sold to you with product after product promising to make you feel like you're good enough. But when you shift your focus to all the other important people and things happening around you in the real world, it becomes clear that there really is no need for you to be perfect in order to have a fulfilling and meaningful life. Nobody is demanding that of you except yourself. Nobody is quite as concerned with your human imperfections as you. Start focusing on what you can do for others and how you can be of service. It is easier to shift the habit of self-criticism if you are not constantly putting yourself under the microscope. What is one thing you can focus on today that would make the lives of your loved ones just a little better?

"Nobody is quite as concerned with your human imperfections as you."

Takeaways

- There is a poisonous set of ingredients that, when added to self-criticism, make it harmful rather than helpful. If your aim is not just to bully yourself but to do better, then crafting self-criticism masterfully will propel you forward rather than holding you back.

- You can be highly disciplined, driven, and productive without constantly bringing yourself down. Self-respect does not lead to a life of indulgence.

- Take a break from self-focus and shift your attention to everything else that matters to you. Too much inward focus will make you feel worse, not better.

- The truth doesn't have to be harsh, and compassion must never be a lie. Honesty must be delivered with skill and careful consideration about which direction you are heading in.

- When you are not trying to grapple with your worthiness as a human being, you are free to get to work learning and improving. So leave the global self-judgments off the table and focus on what it is you are trying to achieve.

CHAPTER 14

When you doubt yourself and want to feel more confident

The only person you are destined to become is the person you decide to be.

—Attributed to Ralph Waldo Emerson

A letter from me to you

This letter might not be quite what you were looking for. But what we look for isn't always what we need. I know that feeling all too well, flicking through the pages of books that promise to make you feel more confident, hoping to find the one book that holds the key to switching that feeling on. Most of those books tell us to eradicate our doubts (which feels impossible to do) and convince ourselves that we already have all the confidence we need (which feels like a lie). But what all of those books miss, and that you discover only through living, is that chasing confidence is not how you find it.

Confidence is not something you aim for and then arrive at. It is just a by-product of a life spent focused on other things. You pick a domain that you want to master, whether it be social interaction, taking exams, football skills, or public speaking. Then, every time you willingly enter the space in which confidence leaves you, whenever you hone your craft or prepare for battle, whenever you win or lose and get back up to go again, there is a tiny incremental strengthening of confidence. Another piece of evidence that when you choose to face what is difficult and holds no guarantee of success, you inevitably survive and learn from it. Whether the outcome appears superficially to be a win or a loss, you have not come away with nothing. Once you truly know that you can survive losing, you can become relentless, and confidence in your own resilience in the face of unpredictable outcomes grows.

In this equation we start with the act; we end with the feeling. But the hard part is the willingness to go there, into the space where we feel vulnerable and can't control the results, and the commitment to stay until we learn all there is to learn.

If you are pushing your limits in the way that's necessary to build confidence, you will feel a spike in anxiety and the urge to back off until you can be certain that everything will be okay. That fear is inherent in the process, and when you choose to look at it that way, the feelings can be tolerated or even embraced rather than perceived as unbearable. Telling yourself that you cannot endure even the temporary discomfort of uncertainty and vulnerability will march you straight down the path toward immediate safety. This is not the path to confidence. The only way to trust in your ability to get through, even when circumstances are less than ideal, is to build up evidence of having done so before.

The key requirement is that you are willing to be the beginner who makes mistake after mistake to learn and improve while contributing where you can. With this mindset you can welcome some of that nervousness as an indication that you are on the right path. This doesn't mean you have to think positively all the time. You don't have to squash all negative thoughts and have 100 percent self-belief. In fact, when you are trying to improve at something, ignoring your vulnerabilities or convincing yourself they don't exist is likely to be a short-lived illusion.

Instead, accept the reality that doubts and vulnerabilities will crop up everywhere when you are facing challenges and focus on your personal commitment to courage, effort, and forward momentum.

One day, you'll look up and see how many situations that you once feared now feel well within the bounds of your comfort zone. But you won't ponder on it for long because by then, your commitment to courage, effort, and forward momentum will be such that you'll be off in search of the next challenge. Enjoy the ride.

Real-time tools

Much of the work that goes on in therapy is a process of confidence building. Not the superficial boost of positivity in fleeting moments, but a deeper, more enduring relationship to the self and the challenges that lie before us. For that, we cannot miss out on the work of pinpointing some of the biggest contributors to persistent poor confidence. Once we know what they are, we can spot them coming, even if it's a subtle manner in which we perceive things. Pulling at the root in this way makes things easier later on.

Pull out weeds from the root

The following are just a few of the possible contributors to weed out whenever you notice them. But identifying the role they play just once is not enough to change it. For such acknowledgment to move the dial, we have to catch it in the moment, when it rears its ugly head. Then you get to choose whether you go with it or do things differently this time. But that won't happen straight away. It usually starts with spotting it after it occurs, perhaps with journaling, attending therapy, or talking with someone. Over time, with enough repetition, you then start to notice it in the moment, as it happens. To start, see if any of these resonate for you, then make a plan to keep a log of when they appear.

Fear of the unknown

Let's just take a moment to normalize the reality that when entering into a new situation you can expect confidence to be low and stress to be high. This is not a problem. It's your brain rightfully identifying that this situation is not familiar (and therefore not easily predictable) and that demands are being made of you. So you get a shot of the stress response that increases your level of alertness and helps you focus on the challenge in front of you.

That is not in any way a sign that the situation or activity is not for you. True confidence is not an overinflated self-belief or arrogance but a realistic inner sense of what you are capable of and the courage to put that to the test. When you lack experience and haven't yet learned the skills you need, or you know you haven't prepared enough, then a lower level of confidence is a fair reflection of reality and a useful signpost telling you where to direct your efforts.

If there is a challenge ahead and you want to go into it with more confidence, get to work. Make a plan to hone your craft and go into the big day with more tools on your belt than you have today. The key is to build upon small challenges incrementally, increasing in difficulty or pressure as you go.

Expectations

If you are willing to turn toward that lack of confidence with curiosity, you can often pick up on what it is telling you. For example, I just mentioned above that it is normal, healthy, and useful to tread new paths with less confidence than the more well-trodden ones. But this lack of confidence will be magnified intensely if the expectations you have for yourself are not balanced with the situation at hand.

If you are comparing yourself with someone who is already part of the way along their own journey and expecting yourself to bring an equivalent performance, a lack of confidence is going to be a fair reflection of reality. But if your expectation for yourself is that you put in something a little extra and go a bit beyond your own performance yesterday, then a genuine feeling of confidence is not only possible but likely.

This is often where perfectionists slip up. The expectations are so unrealistic and unrelentingly high that there is no room left to feel confident. Expectations should be honest about your preparation, proportionate to your ability, and achievable even when they are far-reaching. Building confidence is all about getting your ducks in a row and setting expectations that reflect reality—and the context is a pretty crucial duck not to be missed.

"There is also a distinct difference between not being good enough and not being ready yet. Failure is something we encounter, not something we become."

There is also a distinct difference between not being good enough and not being ready yet. Underprepared and under-trained should never lead to the conclusion that you will never be able to do this. You can come to that conclusion only once you have done everything within your power to get there. So be careful with your language. The word *never* should appear rarely. In fact, be vigilant in your use of language entirely. Language used with precision can unlock new meaning from our situation and become a recipe for action. So take some time to notice the language you are using and acknowledge how it frames your assessment of and emotional reaction to the challenges you face. If you are trying to act with confidence, which often means moving forward through fear and uncertainty, with no guarantee of the outcome, then the focus of your attention needs to be not just positive but productive, something that helps you to move in the direction you intend to go.

Mistaking failure for final judgment

Failure is something we encounter, not something we become. It is an experience, not a personality trait. If you refuse to accept it as a final judgment, it can become a teacher. Every time you ex-perience failure, you are presented with an opportunity. A chance to learn and take that knowledge forward to the next chapter. If the only thing you harvest from a setback is to brand yourself a failure, then you get nothing. You refuse to receive the new insight and wisdom this moment is offering to hand you.

The tendency to condemn ourselves in this way comes as eas-ily as breathing, and within seconds of realizing our mistakes the words fall from our mouths: "Idiot, loser, waste of space." But even as we label ourselves as nothing but a failure, we have not missed the chance to mitigate the damage it can do. So don't let it go unchecked. Catch yourself saying it, even in the privacy of your own mind, and force yourself to provide a counterweight by coming up with a statement that is both a better reflection of reality and a more productive and helpful assertion to fuel your continued efforts toward improvement. I have shared more on how to do this in chapter 13, "When your inner voice is your own worst critic," but let your comeback to such self-loathing be a fierce self-compassion that wants to see you get back up and battle through. This demands accountability, honesty, a focus on how to repair the holes in your performance, and a plan of action to get you moving. There's no place in that recipe for contempt, self-hatred, or shame if you want to do better.

The recipe for confidence building

There is a simple recipe for building confidence, but it must be applied individually to the different fields that you want to master. Whether you want to do better in your studies, a sport, public speaking, or a particular craft, make sure you are following this process for optimal learning and progress.[1]

1. **Put in the reps.** Put in the training and practice the skills that are necessary to master this domain. Every repetition of the process is carving out neural pathways that will allow your brain to automate much of the process for you over time. This is the part where effort is high and progress appears slow if you keep looking for it.
2. **Stress test.** While the reps are at the core of your progress, you can never expect to hop from the gym straight to race day, or from the textbook to exam day. Whether it's

physical muscles or mental ones, put them to the test as regularly as you can. Incrementally add difficulty and pressure to those tests in whatever way you can to mimic the challenges you might face on the pitch, at the track, or in the exam hall. Gradually increase the number of people watching you perform or speak, tighten up the time pressure on practice runs or mock exams. Understanding the aspects of the task that challenge your confidence will guide your choices on this. Constantly challenging your skills will manifest a good pace of progress and no need for major leaps of faith when the big day comes.

3. **Examine each performance.** You could continually put your skills to the test yet repeat the same mistakes over and over with very little learning in between. To get the most out of each challenge, big or small, embrace it as a learning experience. What aspects of your performance do you want to replicate in the future, and which skills need more work? Examine it down to the finest details and treat this as the valuable information that it is. The fruits of this reflection process map out the path toward further progress.

4. **Turn insights into action.** It's no use just saying that you need to execute a certain skill in a slightly different way; your brain will learn only from having the chance to try it out and practice it again and again. If you identify which subject cost you the most deductions on a practice exam paper, take that information and use it. Go back to the beginning with that knowledge and do the reps once again, training these weaknesses in isolation until they become strengths. Then return to step 1 and repeat the process.

Try this: For this quick experiment, it might be helpful to write down your answers so you can refer to them afterward. I want you to take a few moments to imagine that, by some miracle, you woke up and your confidence in yourself had magically blossomed. From the moment you opened your eyes in the morning, how would you know this had happened? When you answer this, try to focus less on how you might *feel* differently and more on exactly what you would *do* differently and how you would do it. How would you hold yourself? How would you move? How might you interact with people differently? How would you approach upcoming challenges? Try to consider the finest details of difference. Paint that picture in your mind and use it to construct a list of actions.

Most people, when they dream in this way, assume that they must wait for that feeling or problem to change before the story can come true. But much like the problem of motivation, confidence is not a feeling that comes first. So everything on the list you have created, those are the actions that will in fact help to invite that feeling. Some things on the list will feel more possible than others. Why not start with those?

Confidence is the bus that never arrives while you sit waiting. It usually makes an appearance after you have decided to walk and you're almost at your destination. So get to work on making some progress, and I'll bet the bus arrives once you're a little ways down the road.

Takeaways

- Don't aim for confidence. You will never arrive. Confidence is a by-product of the willingness to start at the bottom and work your way up, learning as you go. It is a product of failure as well as victories if you continue to learn from each.

- A lack of confidence in new and unpredictable situations is normal and not a reason to withdraw. Rather than trying to eradicate the feeling, focus your attention on learning and contributing in equal measure. Do your best, and when your best falls short, work out ways to do better.

- To build confidence, you must be willing to risk failure. To do that, you must be willing to recognize failure as a necessary part of the learning process. It does not say anything fundamental about your worthiness as a human being. All it tells you is what to work on next.

- Be careful with your language. There is a distinct difference between not being good enough and not being ready yet. Where there is commitment to effort, there is potential for improvement.

CHAPTER 15

When you feel overwhelmed

The best way out is always through.

—Robert Frost, "A Servant to Servants"

A letter from me to you

If it feels like everything is closing in on you and you are losing your ability to think straight about any of it, I'm really glad you have made it here. In this space, for the next few minutes, all you have to do is follow these words. That spotlight of your attention, which has been trying to focus on everything at once, can, for these few moments, narrow right down to just these words. Just you and me. And as these words unfold, let's just slow everything down. Come back to the natural rhythm of your breathing and see if you can fill the lungs a little more deeply and take your time to breathe out slowly. As you do that, you'll notice that each exhale will allow you to sink down a little more and uncoil some of that tension that was there a few moments ago. Now unclench your jaw and rest your tongue on the roof of your mouth. Let your shoulders drop. That's it.

Let's just get clear that this is not the moment to fix everything. In this moment, you need not be anything other than you, as you are now. Let's leave it all in the past and the future where it belongs and scale right back to now. All you need to do is find your balance. The pressure is off for this moment as we pause and invite the whole body to slow down. The tension that was there was unpleasant but not harmful, and you are not at the mercy of it. You will feel a release as we bring that state of tension down to a calm and nurturing rest. A slowing down.

This is not giving up or opting out. This is pressing pause so that you can step off the merry-go-round and recenter, recalibrate. Let the eyes soften and drop your eyebrows, loosening that jaw once again if you need to. As you rest with each long exhale, I have something to tell you.

Some of the most profound changes I have witnessed in people over the years have not been when their lives suddenly got easier. It was when people started to discover that they had more capacity to cope than they ever imagined.

The reason nobody ever taught you the limits of what you can deal with is because nobody knows. Not even you. So when you tell yourself you cannot cope with what is up ahead, know that this thought simply cannot be a fact. It is the narrative you are telling yourself.

And this moment of stillness is not to protect you from the outside world because, well, you don't need protecting. When you choose to take this challenge head-on, you will find the strength that you weren't able to see before, and you will learn what is possible.

"You have more capacity to cope than you ever imagined. A confronting foot forward feels fundamentally different from a recoiling step back."

And every time it all feels too much, that the merry-go-round is spinning too fast, you can return to this space and I'll be here. We can go through the motions to calm the mind and rest a little as many times as you need so that you are ready to get back on and do a little more of everything that matters to you.

The beauty of these moments is that they are small. They don't need to involve any big decisions. The train doesn't have to grind to a halt. Nobody will even notice that you've taken such a tiny moment to yourself, but you will have reclaimed your sense of agency and can return ready to take on just one small step at a time. When you have been overwhelmed by trying to comprehend everything in your path, you stand with a new focus, not on the far horizon but on the next couple of steps in front of you, discovering that when you thought you couldn't manage it, that thought was holding you back.

When the outcome and so much of the situation feels out of your control, rest your newly set horizon on what you know you can influence for the better. Push this thing where it moves. Then start putting one foot in front of the other, honoring the fact that you are not avoiding this, not running from it. A confronting foot forward feels fundamentally different from a recoiling step back. It reveals the strength you didn't know you have for the next step, and the one after that.

Real-time tools

When it comes to using the right tools to help you move through overwhelm, a key distinction to keep in mind is that you can be under intense stress and still preserve a sense of agency.

167

This is the all-important awareness that you can determine your own actions and have influence over your environment. While you still hold on to that, the most important thing you can do is use it. When overwhelm hits, it can be accompanied by a perceived loss of agency and choice. When that happens, then we need to reconnect with a sense of safety, which will give some clarity of thought once again. This next tool is going to help you do that.

Grounding

If you are feeling stuck in a state of immobility or tension, this short exercise gives you a break from overwhelming stimuli and a chance to reconnect with your body in the here and now and reorient to the present moment.

 Try this: Put your feet on the ground as you begin.

Notice what else you can touch nearby. Whether it's your clothes, the wall, or the chair you're sitting on, just take a few moments to explore that thing, as if for the first time.

Observe and then describe in your mind how it feels: the temperature, the texture, the weight of it in your hands.

Now look around and find something in this space that you haven't paid much attention to recently. Maybe because it's not that interesting, just something you tend to pass by without much thought. Spend a few moments getting more familiar with that object, observing and describing it in your mind once again. You might notice how the light falls on it, the colors and shadows, the textures and lines. What words would you use to describe this thing?

Now expand that awareness to pick up on the sounds you can hear. Some of them might come from nearby, others might seem far away. You're not trying to judge or change any of those; simply notice, observe, and then describe them in your mind.

You can keep doing this, looking for things in your immediate environment that you can touch, see, and hear. This is the process of using your senses to bring you back into the present moment when your mind may have taken you off to thoughts that trigger stress and overwhelm.

You can also combine this tool with self-soothing, a great technique for tolerating high levels of distress when you need to get through tough moments. This also involves using each of your senses. But this time you choose to focus on things that you associate with safety and comfort. For example, here in England the ritual of making and sharing tea is so heavily associated with closeness and comfort that when we slow that process down and take notice of each step—paying attention to what we see, hear, and smell as we pour and brew our cup—it can help relieve overwhelm and emotional distress. These soothing sensations can be found in anything, including the perfume of a loved one, a traditional family meal, photographs of happy times, music that calms. You get to choose the details. The key is that you are using each of your senses to bring you into the here and now and soothe your way through distress rather than trying to numb it or escape it.

Check for false narratives that hold you back

Overwhelm occurs naturally in the face of events that threaten to turn our lives upside down, whether it be a death in the family, divorce, or finding ourselves the target of bullying or violence. In these scenarios, overwhelm can happen suddenly. But there are also occasions when overwhelm builds progressively over time. It's not unusual in today's world to experience a gradual increase in the amount of responsibility and demand in one's career at the same time that you also start to build a family. The expectations of what you should be able to manage steadily increase, and the signs of damage caused by chronic stress go ignored until a breaking point occurs.

For others, overwhelm seems less a reflection of the magnitude of the situation and more closely associated with their own estimation of themselves and their apparently limited capacity to deal with stress and painful emotions. Much of my career has been spent working with people through their gross underestimation of the depths of their strength and resilience. "I won't be able to cope" is too often the default and leads to lives that are made smaller and more miserable by decisions based on limiting beliefs.

When people say that you can calm the mind only with the body, that is not accounting for the fact that negative thoughts left unchecked can repeatedly retrigger the stress response and make it feel impossible to remain calm for any significant length of time. So taking a look at the narrative that is feeding the overwhelm is a helpful tool to utilize in the moment. You don't have to challenge it if that feels too much at this point. But notice it and hold it at arm's length. See that script for what it is: a storyline that you can buy into or not. Consider whether you would want

someone you love to buy into though
when they felt overwhelmed. If that lo
the same scenario that you face, how w
rative to sound different? What would y
the strength to see?

You might remember from other chapt
you to try and convince yourself of someth
believe. But every reality has 360 degre
come at the truth from the angle that serv
that don't. This is reframing in action, and y
counteracting those statements such as "I v
These words can be reworked into "How c
to bring my best to this situation in the time t
from trying to avoid what you don't want to a
do want.

Don't identify as a fragile victim

Overwhelm is not an indication of inadequacy
you. It is a signal that the way your life is set up
not working for you or simply that something
your equilibrium. The details of that will be dif
one. It is your job to step away from the temptat
condemn yourself and instead use this as informa
rious about. Start investigating what is contributin
of overwhelm and what your body and mind is
needs. Listen and it will tell you.

No-agenda, non-doing time

Most people are familiar with the feeling that life s
going much faster than the human mind can keep up

Jon Kabat-Zinn, a professor emeritus

lness teacher, puts forward a simple

eems almost radical. He suggests set-

." Protected time in which there is no

being mindful of the present moment.

f the chaos of overwhelm in which the

numb and shut down.[1]

spent alone, but as social beings we are

to community and by connection to the

t is okay to utilize that too. You are being

ng attention to the present moment on

s possible to do that with others.

us system from an active, striving state to

tranquility is going to give some relief from

d replenish your system. Whether it's talking

g to music, walking outside in the fresh air and

me with animals, feeling another's heartbeat,

tion, find what suits you.

efer to follow the sound of someone's voice

editation, you can find some that I have writ-

YouTube channel (@DrJulie), which you can

ou need it.

energy down

rwhelm hits when you're in a state of high ten-

stress, and the need is to bring down that tension

. At other times, the shift needs to go in the other

may be in a low state, but you want to step back

and start meeting the demands placed on you. For

nt to feel more alert and activated, and more able to

focus on the task. Learning how to shift your bodily state up and down in this way is a valuable life tool.

To shift into a state of readiness for action, you can use your breathing, switching from longer exhales to deeper and more vigorous inhales. This will help speed up your heart rate very quickly. You can add to this by using physical movement and carefully chosen music. As you experiment with the various tools, you will become more aware of the impact that each technique has on your physical and emotional state. That awareness is your key to being able to use all these tools to your advantage, whether you need to bring yourself back down to calm, or to activate and energize.

Takeaways

- Feelings are uncomfortable but not dangerous. If you fear the feelings, you will miss what they have to say.

- Experiencing overwhelm does not make you inadequate or disordered, or a victim. It is yet another host of sensations from your body that offers information about what you need. When you are willing to look at that with curiosity, the answers can be simple.

- Resist the temptation to judge and condemn yourself for this. It is not who you are. It is an experience, a set of sensations that each offer information about what you need. Listen to your body, and it will tell you what it needs. Usually the answer is some form of replenishment.

- When overwhelmed, don't let that rapid thought process influence your state without going unchecked. What narrative are you buying into that could be serving to keep you stuck in overwhelm? What alternative script would you need to write for yourself to recalibrate and be ready to move forward?

- Finding calm is not always the state shift we need. Sometimes we need to feel activated and alert, and to move into a readiness for action. Breathwork, physical movement, and music are just some of the ways you can do that. Experiment and get to know what helps you shift into the state you need in the moment.

CHAPTER 16

When you hate who you've become

The self is not something ready-made, but something in continuous formation through choice of action.

—John Dewey

A letter from me to you

Bring to mind someone in your life whom you love without condition. Someone who means the world to you. Someone for whom you want the absolute best. Recall a memory you have of a time you saw them carefree and full of joy. Notice how that image makes you feel.

Now imagine those eyes filled with pain as you hear them say "I hate myself" over and over again. And notice how you feel when you realize that this self-hatred equates with your own.

With every ounce of your being, you want to convince your

loved one of the worthiness and brilliance they cannot see in themselves, because, from the outside, you can see as clear as day that there is so much to love about them. So much to cherish and nurture. If only they could see it too.

Whether they match up to the world's expectations or their own, it does nothing to change your love for them. You can see from the outside that those feelings of self-loathing and self-hatred are no measure of worthiness, because they have it all wrong. You know they are deserving of love and belonging even when they don't recognize it.

Keep that image of you and your loved one. But this time put yourself in their place, and I will stand in yours. I can see from the outside that your self-loathing is nothing but destructive to you. And I see you holding on to it as the only possible truth when I know there is so much more than you can see from where you stand.

Despite my deep yearning to change your mind, no words on this page or any other can erase the experiences that taught you to hate who you are. We cannot close off that path in your mind. We can only forge a new one. A path filled with fierce self-compassion and restitution.

But I am not about to tell you to start chanting "I love you" into the mirror. If you don't like who you are today, your focus must be on who you intend to be tomorrow. Because the good news in all of this is that you are not set in stone, my friend, and the previous chapters of your story do not have to determine the rest. You are one big bag of potential. And the responsibility is all yours to take command of who you are becoming, to treat yourself as a valuable work in progress, even when you don't feel it yet.

You have already seen where the alternative takes you, and it is something you wouldn't wish on anyone else.

Living in line with the person you most want to be, a person you can love, cannot happen until you first treat yourself with respect, compassion, and humility.

To step away from those old narratives is to fiercely commit to having your own back, to wanting the best possible life for yourself and making the best contribution that you can to the world.[1] It means holding in one hand a radical acceptance of the parts of you that you dislike the most, and in the other hand, the kindness and encouragement that you would offer to your loved one we thought about a moment ago. It means taking control of how you treat yourself, how you relate to others, and how you engage with life, even when old habits are dying hard, and knowing that self-loathing goes a long way to keeping you stuck.

Real-time tools

Your estimation of yourself rarely changes overnight. Like most things, it shifts in small, repeated increments over time. In addition to that, it never came to you ready-made. It was molded by many different people, experiences, and actions, many of which you won't even recognize as having made an impact. None of the tools that follow offer the one miraculous game changer. But each will make a considerable contribution to your ability to make careful choices about how you relate to yourself going forward, and to notice the impact those choices have on your life.

"Take command of who you are becoming. If you don't like who you are today, your focus must be on who you intend to be tomorrow."

Don't mask self-loathing with perfectionism

One way that self-hatred shows up in your life is when you seek the wrong relationships, sabotage the ones that could have been healthy, and turn away from opportunities. But it doesn't always look like such obvious self-destruction.

In our efforts to rid ourselves of such psychologically threatening feelings and beliefs, we develop certain rules for living that promise to keep us safe from the reality of those damaging core beliefs. You might tell yourself, "As long as I am liked by everyone around me, then I am okay." So you set to work on making sure that others think you are helpful and kind and worthwhile. This is an impossible task to sustain that will absorb as much energy as you are able to put into it, and more. The exhaustion of this is sad, but the sadder part is that no matter how much everyone else likes you for everything you do, you never fully arrive. You never feel deeply accepted. You still believe, deep down, that it's all conditional. Without the constant effort, you feel undeserving of love and belonging.

Look out for perfectionist tendencies that mask self-loathing but only while you sustain the unsustainable. Making a valuable contribution to your community is a positive step, but it must be backed up with an estimation of yourself that can carry you through imperfection and the ebbs and flows in your relationships with others.

Without the self-compassion part and the commitment to treat yourself in a way that all humans need and deserve, prepare to spend the rest of your life on a treadmill. Because without those you will never feel enough. You will simply find new measuring sticks that put your ability to feel happiness and contentment in the perpetual future.

Take yourself by the hand, educate yourself, and start engaging fully in the world, knowing that you offer yourself a place of belonging to return to, always.

It's important not to blur the boundaries between modesty and self-denigration. Treating yourself as unimportant and of no consequence feeds that self-loathing and all its destructive actions. Those actions will then at best blemish and at worst destroy all that matters to you from the center to each small corner of your life.

Your tendency to direct hate toward yourself is not a sign of your worthiness. It gives you no information about whether you are lovable and deserving of happiness and fulfillment. But it is a sign that change needs to happen for you to get the most out of your life. It demands partly a closing of the gap between the person you are living as and the person you want to be. But relentless self-improvement alone will not fill the void of self-loathing. It might just mask it to you and others. The key is in appreciating and taking care of yourself like a child who needs a sense of belonging and encouragement, truly looking out for yourself and your future as if you were really someone you cared about. That ensures that you don't need to delay happiness and contentment until the day you become this elusive perfect self that none of us ever arrive at. Aspire to it, but be okay with not being entirely there, and you'll be in good company throughout the whole journey.

Make a commitment, now, to speak to yourself in a way that ensures the best possible outcome for you. At this point it doesn't matter if you believe you deserve it. What matters is knowing that this is what you must do to start changing your life in the way you want it to change.[2]

Don't give in to emotional reasoning

Many people assume that we think and feel quite separately, that feelings are the irrational, chaotic side of us, while our thoughts represent a rational counterpart. This is not nearly as true as we would like. Much of what we think has been crafted by how we feel, and those thoughts in turn have their own impact on how we feel.

An emotion is your brain's best guess about the meaning of the moment. But it rarely has access to all the facts. So it fills in the gaps with memories of similar scenarios from the past and other information from your body about whether all is well. When you understand this about emotions, it becomes easier to see how we all make a habit of emotional reasoning. This is when we feel something and, rather than see that as just one possibility, take it as evidence of fact. *I feel it, therefore it must be true.*

Once you know about emotional reasoning, you'll see it everywhere. But it's easier to spot in others than yourself. There are a thousand reasons why you might feel stupid in a given moment. But concluding that you are dumb and useless despite evidence to the contrary would be emotional reasoning. Most people in the world have been made to feel worthless at some point. But you would never suggest to someone that feeling it makes it so. Yet many take that feeling and assume that they are, indeed, worthless. The real damage occurs when we then start to act in line with that conclusion. If you see yourself as worthless, you are going to behave as such in everything you do. Even the smallest of negative emotions will seem more significant than they truly are and will be used to reconfirm what an apparent lowlife you have assumed you are.

None of this steers you in the direction that would make your life better. Developing the ability to spot emotional reasoning gives you a fighting chance at stopping it in its tracks.[3]

Choose the narrative

If you are going to have the courage to take on all the things that are currently making your life worse, then language matters. Go back to the image of the person you love without condition. If you wouldn't say it to them, don't say it to you. And if the thought arises from years of habit, never let it go unchecked.

Every time you are served up the narrative of self-loathing, you know where that takes you, and it's not pretty. It's not the best option for you or anyone you love. Have you ever benefited from someone else's self-hatred? No. But it's possible you have been harmed by it.

The narrative of self-hatred might sound like a version of the story that turns you into the villain, assumes other people feel contempt for you, and suggests you deserve the bad things that happen to you. It also sounds like you convincing yourself to hold back from making a well-intentioned and imperfect contribution to your world because your mind is a frightening place to be if you fail. When you notice such scathing self-attacks turn up, take a moment to write them down, which will help reduce their status from unquestionable facts to a biased echo of the past that is of no help to your future.

Don't squash anger, make use of it

If you start to experience anger, I'd say that is good news. Anger often needs a sprinkling of self-worth in order to show up. It's the anger that you would feel for the people who had convinced your loved one to hate themselves. Anger is not as bad as we have all been led to believe. As long as it is not turned against the self or on anyone who is not actively harming you, it can be a driving force. Anger is a command to action. It's the fire in you to haul yourself up and make things better. Don't numb it. Use it as fuel, and it won't hang around. It will take its natural course.

Map out the past to understand how you got here

While it is difficult to challenge painful core beliefs, a powerful way to get some distance from the feelings so that you can see them for what they are is to understand the aspects of your story so far that made this pattern likely to develop. This can help us to remind ourselves in the moment that the sensitivity of old wounds is not always the best version of reality today. That sensitivity protected you when you needed it. But eventually it can become a destructive force in your life.

The most intelligent and insightful of people can carry the most unsound core beliefs about themselves that will override logic. We base decisions on emotion and rationalize it afterward. So transformation starts with understanding the faulty learning that set up these beliefs in the first place. This might be caused by one distinct trauma. It may be a more subtle and slow erosion of the self that is impossible to see with perspective until you are old enough to live outside the family system and look in with a new knowledge of how others do it differently.

The next stepping-stone to firmer ground is telling the story—putting words to the images from your own mind, either by writing or talking in a safe space. By looking back at those early experiences once you are no longer there and no longer dependent, you can revisit them in a constructive way that helps you enhance your perspective on the consequences that you still deal with today. Trace all the ways your mind took on those beliefs to help keep you safe and how your mind continues on that loop with the same intention. Through this new learning, you'll discover that the loop is no longer necessary.

Putting that story on the outside of your mind, looking down on it with a bird's-eye view, itself has a transformative effect. It's much easier to see where paths lead when you are flying over the woods, as opposed to walking through them. You get a map of where you've been, where you're going wrong, and which way to go next.[4]

Master your mind

Given that we cannot control the thoughts that pop into our mind, how do we master it? What we don't want is you attacking yourself for attacking yourself. That is a pointless cycle. Get into the habit of noticing what you are thinking. A daily mindfulness practice will train the mental muscles needed to do this. When you notice a thought that sounds like something you wouldn't say to a friend, then block it from going any further. This is not the same as trying to make it go away. It is finding a counter-response from the part of you that is looking to a better future and no longer has time for kicking yourself while you're down.

You can respond out loud or in your own mind with *No. That type of comment is not helpful. I don't speak to myself like that anymore. It only takes me down.* You can also add a reality check in which you challenge the validity of that thought, but only if it is quick and easy. You don't want to get into a tussle with self-critical thoughts. You want to quickly nip them in the bud by recognizing them for what they are, an echo of the past that is only going to hold you back if you spend time with it.

Then turn toward the new voice that you have identified as the one you need. The one that helps you haul yourself up and push forward. It might be the firm and supportive coach, the loving parent, or your compassionate self. You can develop that voice over time, but it needs to be unapologetic, unwavering in its support, 100 percent committed to the best possible future for you. Get ready for this to feel uncomfortable, cringeworthy, self-indulgent, and silly. All the old judgments about why kindness is so ridiculous will echo from the past, loud and clear, making it hard to stay committed. But it doesn't have to instantly feel right for it to be the thing that you need in the long run. Acknowledge those echoes as an extinction burst of those old narratives and stay committed while they subside.[5]

Takeaways

- You did not learn to hate yourself overnight, and unlearning it will take time too. But it is work that must be done if you are to break free from self-loathing and the misery it causes.

- Perfectionism will only mask self-hatred if your respect for yourself remains highly conditional. Aiming high and striving to make a contribution is a positive, but you must treat yourself like someone you value in the face of both victory and defeat.

- Emotional reasoning (*I feel it therefore it is true*) is a common bias that is your enemy as you do this work. Don't let it slip past without challenging its assumptions.

- It's okay to feel angry if your life is not where you want it to be. Just be sure to use that anger to your advantage. Channel it in a carefully chosen direction and use it to fuel positive action. Anger indiscriminately directed at the self will pull you down.

CHAPTER 17

When you're scared of making the wrong choice

It's not hard to make decisions when you know what your values are.

—Roy E. Disney

A letter from me to you

A fork in the road doesn't always feel quite like the opportunity that it is. Fear of making the wrong choice can keep you rooted to the spot. So you start looking for all the reasons for that fear. And when you look, you will find. Once you know what you're afraid of, there is relief in putting off the decision, at least for now. But every course of action incurs some form of cost and something that must be tolerated or let go. But fixating on those alone is a mistake. It fails to acknowledge the deep emptiness and, later on, despair that can come from never having taken any action at all.

Some choices are just difficult. There are no perfect decisions, only lots of imperfect ones. Every path has a price to pay, a letting go of something that might have been. While there are some regrets we can't see coming, others we can predict ahead of time. In making decisions about how you will live your life and what you will aim for, acknowledge the regrets inherent in each path. All we can do is choose the regrets we can live with, the ones that we could be at peace with later, not the ones that will leave us grieving for a life that could have been more meaningful.[1]

Of course, life never feels quite so simple as weighing up two potential futures and seeing which one comes out on top. Our idea of what defines "better" is pulled in different directions. What we want and what we need don't always match. And the people we are responsible for bring their own contradictory needs. So the idea of the best choice gets complicated and laced with outcomes both good and bad that you can't predict.

The only way to summon the courage to make big decisions is to commit to forgive yourself when you take a wrong turn.

No one can make this decision for you. But that is good news. It means you cannot be a victim of the outcome. You have the chance to take control of this aspect of your life and influence where it goes. Committing fully to your choice, whether it turns out to be right for you or not, is always a gain if you are willing to learn and shift direction as you need to. That winding path becomes the adventure of your life.

Real-time tools

There are things you can do that help make complex choices simpler to navigate. Some of these are quick exercises you can do in the moment. Others are skills to practice and build on in the longer term.

What matters most

It is much harder to make decisions when we are being pulled in different directions that seem to contradict each other. So it makes sense to work out how much weight to give to each of those influences. Our values and priorities change as we go through life, and a brief check-in with those is always a good idea when there is a big decision to be made. There are different ways to do this, which I cover in more detail in my first book (see chapter 33 of *Why Has Nobody Told Me This Before?*). But when you are focused on a specific decision, this is an easy way to make sure that your choice is based on what matters most to you at this point in your life.

 Try this: Write down a list of the different aspects of your life that are likely to be affected by the decision you face. Examples include family, parenting, friendships, intimate relationships, career, health, education, personal development, community, and contribution.

Next to each of these different areas, write down a few words in answer to the following questions:

- What is most important to you about this area of your life?
- How do you most want to show up and contribute here?
- How will the choice that you face affect your capacity to live in line with these values? Will it bring you more in line with them or further away?

- How will you feel about that? Will that enhance
  your life or diminish it?

  Depending on the gravity of the situation you are facing and the different values that it conflicts with, you can spend as little or as much time with this as necessary. The only requirement is that you are willing to be truly honest with yourself in the process. Not as easy as it sounds. Often, the answers we get are not the ones we want to hear. Especially if we realize that the choice we need to make is the most difficult one.

Boons and pitfalls

When a person comes to therapy and they are contemplating change, but so far have been unable to commit to it, we work with them to break it down in a way that people don't always make time for in day-to-day life.

When we are contemplating making a change, but so far have been unable to commit to it, we might weigh up the advantages and disadvantages of the change. We can see clearly if benefits outweigh the costs. But then we can't understand why we still feel hesitant to start. This simplistic analysis has missed something crucial.

Something that we all seem to overlook is the payoffs of doing nothing. The ways in which *not* taking action on this choice rewards you and allows you to avoid something. Once you have identified those payoffs, you can get honest with yourself about what inaction is costing you and will continue to do so over a lifetime.

 Try this: This is an insightful exercise when you already know the choice you need to make but have been avoiding taking action on it. You can use the following questions as prompts.

- What are the payoffs in holding back on this decision?
- What does it allow you to avoid?
- What does that cost you now and in the future?
- Are you willing to live with the consequences of that?

Tolerate doubt

With all this focus on committing to a choice, it should be pointed out that making your decision will not necessarily put an end to the anguish. You may not instantly believe that this was the best possible decision you could have made for yourself. The doubt may continue. If you need to reassess, then do so constructively, but don't allow yourself to ruminate on the paths you didn't choose, especially if you didn't choose them for good reason. The presence of doubt does not make it the wrong choice. It can mean that you are simply feeling the losses from the sacrifices you made for this path to work. Keep your eyes on where you are going, not where you might have gone.

Failure

If you often experience some form of decision-making paralysis, then looking into your personal relationship with failure is a good place to start.

There will be people in your life who have made you feel afraid to fall and others who have made you feel like you could fly, simply by their response to you in success and failure. No failure hurts more than one that is followed by a stream of abuse that causes you to question your self-worth.

When we have learned to expect that kind of verbal ham-

"Keep your eyes on where you are going, not where you might have gone."

mering for getting things wrong, we find ourselves unable to make a decision. And that is also the case when that hammering comes from you. The most potent way to find courage in the face of big decisions is to know, without a doubt, that you will have your own back when you fail. That is not an *if* but a *when*. Because of course you will fail somewhere along the line.

But when you commit to truly looking after yourself in the face of failure, as if you were someone you believed in and truly cared about—when you bring the words that you need to hear, instead of echoing past bullies—then hauling yourself back up becomes easier. It feels less like being pushed down and a little more like being given a hand up.

To be able to trust that you will respond to failure in a way that helps, whether it's in the role of the protective friend you need or the coach who wants you to find your limits, you need to get serious about it. Find the words, plan them out, listen to what lifts you and what brings you down. You are not losing. You are living. You are learning. You are witnessing yourself get back up every time. With that, the fear of failure stalks you less and less.

Takeaways

- Lingering doubt is not always a reason to stop. If you have given a decision careful thought and it is in line with your most fundamental values, then tolerating the uncertainty of not knowing how it will all work out becomes a part of the process. Doubt can come along for the ride, but it doesn't get to make your decisions for you.

- If you know you've made the right choice but can't seem to take action, spend a little time exploring the payoffs of keeping things as they are. What is inaction helping you to avoid? And what is it going to cost you? Is that something you're willing to endure?

- How have you been taught to view failure? Is that holding you back from making certain decisions? When you feel most brave to make choices, how is failure presented in those contexts?

- Failure is both inevitable and easier to recover from when we have someone by our side whom we can trust to have our backs. How would your life change if you decided to do that for yourself?

CHAPTER 18

When you're short on willpower

Remember the airplane takes off against the wind, not with it.

—Attributed to Henry Ford

A letter from me to you

Sometimes it can feel like two parts of yourself are yearning for different things. One part of you knows exactly what would be best for you in the long-term. But another part of you can't bear the thought of starting today. So you don't. You promise yourself you'll start tomorrow. But when tomorrow comes, the same internal conflict continues, and so that thing you know will benefit you gets put off yet again in favor of older, easier habits.

A struggle with willpower doesn't just occur when the task is especially punishing or painful. Take exercise, for example: most people know that once they get started, they quite enjoy themselves and feel better afterward. But it's not the task that is difficult. It's often the friction we feel between a state of not doing and doing. Once you have momentum, willpower no longer feels like a necessary component. But building momentum takes huge amounts of both physical and psychological effort as you strain against resistance.[1]

If you are a little way into this problem, you'll probably recognize that the tendency to dress up the choice not to start is just a temporary delay as you await better conditions. When you have more time, feel less tired, have fewer things on your mind. But as time goes on, you realize that there are always plenty of reasons to delay. You always have responsibilities that are competing for priority, and you never feel perfectly ready to begin. The deferred action feeds that continued battle in your own mind and the inevitable regret later down the road.

But knowing that regret is inevitable in the distant future doesn't make the current friction any more tolerable. You are always more connected to how you feel now than to how you might feel later. The real energy to push forward comes when you realize that there will always be an opposing force. When you are aiming up, friction is inherent in every move you make.

So don't wait to feel like it. Don't wait for the perfect time. If the goal in your mind truly matters to you, just start moving in that direction. However small the first steps need to be, they are the building blocks of momentum.

As the bestselling author Steven Pressfield so rightly pointed out, the real game, the real battle, is you against the resistance.[2] And when you commit to lean into the resistance and to edge forward in the face of it, you get to relish the pride of taking a stand and choosing your direction instead of being pushed downhill. Nothing will make you feel more alive than aiming up, pushing forward, and witnessing yourself start to move.

Real-time tools

If you want to start building habits that pave the way toward your goals, this section is filled with tools that all have a role to play in creating an environment in which willpower can thrive. While each tool has evidence behind it, you might find some more suited to you than others.

Ask yourself some tough questions

One mistake most people make when trying to find the willpower to act is to pay heed to the trends promoted online that involve visualizing how wonderful everything could be once you reach the end point of a goal, imagining you are already there, and reminding yourself of all the reasons you want to achieve it. While there is some merit in that, a less gentle but somewhat potent tool for activating yourself is to also get real about two things:

1. The payoffs you experience for not starting today, that serve to keep you stuck. This means acknowledging that you hold on to a situation you no longer want, not just because it's hard to make the change, but because there's a strong pull to keep things the same. In choosing something new, you may also have to let go of something.
2. The true consequences for you in keeping things the same. Inherent in this is the acknowledgment that not yet choosing to change is still very much a choice. This enables you to fully engage with the consequences of today's actions, rather than perceiving it as merely a delayed choice.

Try this: Spending a few minutes writing down your answers to these questions can help you gain clarity on the push and pull we can often feel between the prospect of change and keeping things the same.

- In holding back, what are you protecting yourself from? What are the downsides of this change that you are avoiding?
- What benefits or comforts do you enjoy now that you would have to let go of when you take action?
- What gains are you missing out on when you don't take action?
- What is it costing you personally every time you choose to keep things the same?
- If you don't see this through or you fail to even begin, what will that mean for you?
- How will that affect your estimation of yourself?
- How will it affect the things in your life that matter most to you?

Predict your failure

When we are trying to make positive change and we face temptation from the options we need to avoid, and a reluctance to take action that we know will benefit our future, we can learn a lot from the most extreme cases of this work: addictions. For those in treatment for addictions, a significant amount of time is spent on relapse prevention. This means planning for the worst days, anticipating all the potential hurdles, and creating a detailed, concrete plan to tackle each one. Without doing this early on, you leave your future in the hands of your impulses.

When something is difficult enough to require willpower, this work will undoubtedly be a worthwhile investment of your time. List all possible threats to your success. This is the time to use self-doubt to your advantage. Allow those worst-case scenario thoughts to run riot for a few moments, knowing that this is part of a more constructive process than simply ruminating on them. We are about to round them up and cage them in with a strong and well-thought-out plan to prevent each one from sabotaging your goals.

Building a plan to minimize chances of failure can require some difficult decisions on your part. It might involve saying no to things that you previously enjoyed or valued, and saying yes to new change that fills you with fear and uncertainty. Rather than allowing this to deter you from the effort ahead, keep the reasons for this goal front and center in your mind. Maintain absolute clarity on why you want this and why you *don't* want the alternative.

 Try this:

- What are the barriers and obstacles ahead that pose a risk to your success?
- What are the times, places, or situations that, if left to impulse, would create a roadblock to your progress?
- What are all the excuses and justifications you might use to make it feel more acceptable to slip off track in those moments?

Once you have a list of all the potential barriers, set about creating a plan of action for how you intend to navigate each one.

While this is an uncomfortable process, what is more anxiety provoking is not knowing what's coming. Running into hurdles full force because you didn't see them coming diminishes your chances of seeing your goal through. But being brave enough to look ahead at the things that are going to bring challenges, and the way you would approach them that would bring about failure, means that when the time comes, you just have to follow the plan for navigating them without too much disruption to your forward momentum.

Prepare to succeed

There are several basic ingredients that make up the recipe for action toward your goals. But they frequently get lost among the demands of everyday life. You would never expect to produce bread without flour, and you cannot expect to bring your best without adding in enough rest. As you begin on your mission, keeping up your willpower will require an adequate amount of time for sleep and replenishment after exertion. Ask any professional athlete, and their commitment to rest will surprise you. No muscle can repair and strengthen without it, and neither can any mind. What might also surprise you is how quickly you can feel the difference when you add in small moments during the day to recharge.

While some would agree that words are power, there is little I could say that would make an underslept, overstressed you spontaneously jolt into action with a high-voltage surge of energy. Saying the right things while withholding the right fuel is not going to roar any engine into life. Some of the mindset-shifting tools in this section will help you push through today. But if what you want is willpower to try again tomorrow and the next day, then you must commit to giving your body and your brain what they need to keep going.

"Commit to effort above all else, as it is the one thing you can control."

Exercise, nutrition, and sleep will amplify your willpower. Without getting these core ingredients right, everything else will feel more difficult. We don't have to get it perfect, but we ignore them at our peril. If you can do one thing today to improve on one of those, you're heading in the right direction and making the whole thing easier for yourself.

Make friends with stress

One key to maximizing willpower is to understand the role of stress in this equation.[3] If your goal involves trying to stop doing something, then you might be interested to know that the higher your stress levels, the more likely you are to give in to temptation. Holding back from something that has been a bad habit for a long time demands a great deal of cognitive effort. But when you feel stressed, that usually means the demands placed on you are exceeding the resources you think you have at that moment. This is when your brain makes use of automated responses as shortcuts to gain comfort or relief from the stress.[4]

Much of that stress may be caused by the outside world, but be aware of the extra stress you add to the system with the narrative of thoughts you give your attention to. If you load up on self-loathing and self-criticism after each setback or slip up, you are unknowingly increasing stress and ramping up the subsequent urges for immediate gratification all the while bringing down your defenses that are necessary to withstand temptation.

Equally, when you are feeling lethargic and trying to kick-start some goal-directed action, stress is important here, too, in a slightly different way. When you start to think about how deeply you want to achieve your goal, you anticipate the pleasure of getting there, and start to feel energized to get going. That sensation is your stress response. It's the one you wanted and the one you need to achieve this goal, but for many it can be an uncomfortable shift from relaxed and restful to slightly agitated and uneasy. Couple that with the uncertainty and anxiety about whether you can do this, and many people have the urge to numb it with something else. If we want to feel energized to strive toward those goals, we need to recognize the utility of that restlessness and take the opportunity to welcome it and channel it in the right direction.

When you feel that friction in switching from rest to movement, calm to energized, safe to uncertain, remind yourself that this is inherent in the process of turning boredom into adventure. The urge to maintain the original state is normal but can be overridden if you're willing to tolerate the feeling and be open to change. In the seconds before you jump into cold water, notice how your mind will recoil at the idea and try to talk you out of it. It's those people who have been in the water for just a few minutes who say "It's quite nice once you get used to it." The initial change in state is always a shock to the system. Once you are in motion, it never feels as bad as you anticipated.

Connect with your future self

Absorbed in all the demands of day-to-day life, most of us never take the time to think too far into the future. It all feels far away and less relevant than everything on our plate right now. Even when you imagine yourself in the future, it often plays out as if you were watching someone else in a movie. The image of that future self feels vague and hard to imagine, but we assume it will be a better version of ourselves that has mastered the challenges of today and is living in a time when everything is easier.

Studies have shown that when we feel disconnected from our future self in this way, we are more likely to disregard the future consequences of today's actions. We tend to be more impulsive and make choices based on how we want to feel now, not what we want for our future. But strengthening that sense of continuity between who you are now and you in the future helps us feel more willing to put in the work today.[5]

If you are disconnected from your future self, you will tend to be more impulsive and make choices based on how you want to feel now, not what you want for your future. If we don't want to mistreat our future selves and give them more to deal with through today's impulsive decisions, it helps to get in touch with the realization that the image of you in the future is not an idealized version of you with no challenges. In fact, effort will feel, in the deepest sense, very much the same as it feels today.

 Try this: Take a few moments to close your eyes and imagine yourself a week or a month from now, looking back on the choices you are making today.

How does your future self feel about those actions? How will they have affected your future?

Now see if you can write a note to that future self and tell them what you are going to do now to make life better for them. What do you need to take action on today to make sure that you in the future looks back with pride and gratitude and a new sense of momentum toward better things?

Takeaways

- Give up the illusion that your future self will somehow have it easier and instead connect with that future self as very much you, as you are now. If you are living fully, there will always be a list of priorities competing for your time and attention. The resistance you feel now will be just as present in the future, so you might as well start today.

- Commit to effort above all else, as it is the one thing you can control.

- Get familiar with the role stress plays in this so that you can use it to your advantage.

- Get to know the payoffs that come with not taking action on something that matters to you, as well as the costs. This will give you a deeper insight into what is keeping you stuck.

- It is naive to assume that when you do start, it will be smooth sailing. The people who succeed in the long-term anticipate what could cause them to fail and make plans for how to navigate challenges. Leave nothing to impulse.

- Willpower does not appear out of thin air; it is a rocket that needs plenty of fuel. Any effort spent on getting more sleep, exercise, and planning a few decent meals is going to help you sustain your efforts for the long haul.

CHAPTER 19

When you must perform under pressure

When we long for life without trials and work without difficulties, remind us that oaks grow strong in contrary winds and diamonds are made under pressure.

—Attributed to Peter Marshall

A letter from me to you

Here it is, right in front of you. An opportunity to put into practice everything you have worked so hard on. You feel pressure on all sides, and when you give it your full attention, you notice that it risks disrupting your ability to concentrate on the process. You start to question your confidence in yourself and your ability to make the right decisions in the moment. You doubt your capacity to remember everything and to keep your cool—all those things that come naturally when pressure is not a part of the equation.

Ask anyone who has ever achieved anything, and they will be no stranger to this feeling. Their ability to bring their best through it all is not a trait they were born with. It's something they learned, as will you.

Whatever the challenge, you have to be as laser-focused on the mindset you bring to it as you have been with every other part of the preparation process. If you give your thoughts free reign, you may think yourself out of performing at your best. If you approach this challenge as a threat, like a rabbit in the headlights, you will feel every bit the prey, not the predator. And if you feel like the prey, you will respond like one: purely focused on surviving a terrifying experience and wishing it over so that you can recover from the stress and tend to any wounds in the form of failure and humiliation. If you do that, you will never fully commit to the job at hand. Your mind will dart this way and that, just like that helpless rabbit in the headlights, frantic to avoid catastrophe and escape the stress of it all. This is not a recipe for your best performance. It's a recipe for confirming all your limiting self-beliefs and the urge to give up on all those ambitions you have.

If your best is what you are going for, then your mind needs to be calibrated so it is in line with your intentions. The prey is focused purely on protecting itself. The predator has its eye on something exciting and will enjoy giving everything to reach its goal. It is that anticipation for the chase that sparks acceleration into the pursuit. The predator who pauses too long to question what might happen, and how she will feel if she doesn't succeed, has already sealed her fate. The thrill of the chase fuels the whole thing. The process may still be grueling and fraught, but you know that without it this would be nothing more than an easy meal. So you embrace the work and the sense of power that ensues.

"If your best is what you are going for, then your mind needs to be calibrated so it is in line with your intentions."

When you direct the spotlight of your attention on all the things that could go wrong and what might happen when they do, it leaves no space to devote to the task ahead of you. But in the same respect, when every inch of your attention is absorbed by the process of this task, there is no space left for overthinking the outcome. The only useful time to put the spotlight on the outcome is after it happens. Before that point, it is the process that needs your full commitment and focus. Think less about how it will feel when you succeed or fail and more about how you will feel when you are executing the process most effectively. Get familiar with that feeling and choose it; wear it like a jacket you wrap around yourself on the way to get the job done. A feeling of vitality as you stride toward your goal, rather than a trembling fear that would have you skirting around the edges of your best self. That jacket is you, feeling good about who you are, the work you have put in, and your reasons for doing so. It's your awareness that, whatever the outcome of this one particular thing, you will strive to reach the next challenge, and the next, because this is just one part of a much bigger picture. Just one chance among many to do your best and learn some more. That is the only path to better things.

The benefits of shifting your focus from the outcome to the process go beyond the impact it can have on your performance. Unwavering self-confidence and life satisfaction are not waiting patiently for you at the finish line. When you arrive there after completing this challenge, or indeed the next, you will realize that you feel much the same as you do now. Those feelings of confidence come when you are absorbed in the chase, when you stretch your legs and discover that the limits you thought you could see firmly staked in the ground up ahead were nothing but a mirage.

When that happens, it is because you've given it everything. You can turn a high-pressure situation caused by something terrifying into something you can enjoy; you achieve this by putting in the hours, doing the work, and getting to know the job inside and out. On the day when you finally step into that arena for real, you're not trying anything new for the first time. No surprises. You are repeating what you have already done a thousand times, so you can enjoy the chance to show off all the work you've put in behind closed doors.

And the pounding heart and sweaty palms will be your signal that your brain has prepared your body to bring your best. You now have a heightened sense of awareness and all that rocket fuel injected into the right places to make this happen. Use it. Don't try to switch that off. It might be agitating and uncomfortable, but it's going to get you where you want to go.

Whatever your personal arena looks like, fully commit to standing tall as you take your place, knowing that, at a fundamental level, you are in competition with no one but your past self.

Real-time tools

As I mentioned at the beginning of this chapter, performing under pressure is a skill you can learn. I'm going to run through a few of those key techniques for you now. If your big day is sooner rather than later, these are skills you can put into practice right away. But you will benefit much more if you put some time and effort into them. The more you do things this way, the more it will become second nature.

What to do about anxiety

Now you might be disappointed to discover that this section does not contain a tool that promises to cure anxiety. Believe it or not, you are going to need that increase in your alertness, reaction speed, and energy coursing through your muscles to get the job done and perform at your best.

What we do need here is a change in how you relate to that anxiety when it shows up to help you. All the time that you are focusing on your pounding heart and trying to make anxiety go away, it is stealing your attention from the thing you came here to do. But the thing about anxiety is that when you allow it to be there, welcome it even, then it tends not to hold you back. You can accept the discomforts and sensations that come with it, knowing that it is enabling you to perform. The key here is to acknowledge that the anxiety will bring with it the urge to step back and withdraw to find safety and calm. Turning toward everything that could go wrong and giving those worst-case scenarios in your mind the time of day will bring about the urges to avoid the situation altogether.

But the fight-or-flight response offers you another option—to fight. This doesn't mean you start swinging. You channel the fear forward, choosing to focus on what you will do when this goes well and how you plan to make it happen.

Watch your language

Whatever your challenge, your best performance is going to be led by a feeling. But for that to happen, you must choose that feeling carefully. And for you to create that feeling, your language is the most powerful ingredient you have. You can't rise without it. In explaining the previous tool, I spoke about anxiety in a way that is likely to come from a very different angle to what you have been used to. This is reframing in practice.[1] Reframing is not lying to yourself or trying to convince yourself of something you don't believe. It is choosing to look at a situation from the perspective that is most helpful to you. It's the predator over the prey, excitement over anxiety, challenge over threat, gratitude over resentment, continuous improvement over limiting self-judgment. These seemingly slight shifts will see you striding into this challenge from a whole new direction, with a different stride, a laser focus, and the capacity to enjoy the process.

I mentioned in my previous book the advice often given online about chanting sweet nothings to yourself that you don't yet believe in. That is not helpful and is likely to set up an argument within your own mind about whether it is true or not. When you repeat a statement that is trying to convince yourself of something, your mind will come up with all the reasons you don't think it's true, further distracting you from the focus you need to perform at your best. That being said, having a few relevant words to anchor you to your chosen focus of attention and emotion state is going to help keep you on track when pressure threatens to distract you.

If you choose to use an affirmation, then it is worth taking some time to make sure it is going to be what you need to hear at the time. Here is a list of pointers to follow when creating an effective affirmation that will help you to bring your best in the tough moments.[2]

- If you don't believe it, then it won't work. Base everything you say to yourself on facts, not feelings or opinions. Choose those facts carefully to have the desired effect on how you feel.

- Words have power when they are backed up by hard work. It's asking a lot of a few words of encouragement to override a lack of preparation. If you're going into something knowing that you haven't put in the work, then adjust your words to reflect what you can expect of yourself at this stage of your learning. At this point, keep in mind that approaching this challenge feeling underprepared is a learning experience in itself. This event is not the end point of your progression. It's a rung in the ladder that will lead to the next. On the other hand, if you have given everything to get to this point, acknowledging your commitment and hard work in your affirmation can help to push your shoulders back and your chin up so that you stride into this with confidence.

- While the best affirmations are instructional and guide your focus and actions, you're not writing a recipe book here. Choose words that make you feel it for real. After all, that's what an affirmation is for. It should induce the mindset and emotion state that you need in order to bring your best and also act as a guide for your focus during the process.

- Use your past success stories to remind yourself of what you do and how you do it when you bring your best to the table. What mindset and attitude do you bring, where do you lock in your focus, and what are those minute details of the way things are done? Through all your hard work up until this point you will undoubtedly have learned that when you do certain things in a certain way, and when you bring some particular personal strengths to the forefront, they all contribute to performing at your best. These are the things to include in your statement to yourself: words that invite you into that zone so that a flow state can take over.

What to do with all those thoughts

As you might well know by now, you can't stop anxious thoughts from arriving. Your mind involuntarily offers up a little prediction about how things might go, and it just happens to sound like a very personal kind of horror story. Simply telling yourself not to think about all the potential negative outcomes means that you are already thinking of them by default.

In addition to the problem of being unable to stop those thoughts from arriving, once they appear, you can't simply remove those unhelpful thoughts from your mind and leave it empty. You must occupy the space with something else. Something that will steer your attention, emotion state, and actions in the direction you want them to go. This is where the affirmations I just described come in.

But sometimes these sorts of tools can sound too good to be true or oversimplified. In reality, we often don't even realize our thoughts have become unhelpful until we are already wrapped up in anxiety and deciding to quit. You can make use of these tools only if you are aware enough to notice whenever your mind has drifted off in that dangerous direction and to show great command in choosing to place your attention on your chosen perspective. This is where preparing and rehearsing your thought process as much as the physical task will help to prevent extra pressure from taking you by surprise and rocking your usual performance on the day.

The most helpful idea I have come across that I use when the pressure is on, and which I referred to earlier in this chapter, is the idea that the focus of my attention is a spotlight. All of the different thoughts and feelings that may pop up and be available to me at any given moment are not fully within my control. But what I do have command of is control of the spotlight of my attention. Just like actors on a stage, the characters to which I give the limelight will change how the story unfolds. The good news is that when we practice, our ability to do this is strengthened. The ability to make this conscious decision about where you place your attention is essentially mindfulness. Every time you engage in mindfulness practice, you are strengthening your capacity to use this powerful real-time tool to get in your zone and bring your best to the table when you most need to.

Steady the body to calm the mind

When you are about to jump in the deep end of a make-or-break situation and you don't feel in your zone, another powerful way to get your mind in the right place is to take control of your physiological response. This does not mean calming the body entirely, as you need the adrenaline and all the heightened awareness you get from this stress response. But you can deliberately slow down your breathing to stop those sensations from escalating and to keep your pounding heart on a rhythm you can handle.

In addition to this, take some time to plan how you intend to use your body to reinforce your mindset and thought-process. The relationship of influence between your body and mind goes both ways. This means how you present yourself and move your body either confirms what you want to be feeling or not. Are you physically showing up in a way that convinces you that you're here to deliver your best? Does it amplify your confidence or diminish it? Sports are a great example of this. Take any of your favorite elite athletes and watch them closely as they walk onto their stage ready to perform. You will not see panicked eyes darting around the crowd as they crouch to bite their nails. You see poise and focus in the face, shoulders low and pushed back, physical posture that is strong yet loose, ready for action, and the purposeful style of movement that comes with a clear vision and a well-prepared plan of action.

The details of how to use your body in this way will depend a great deal on the challenge you're stepping into. You might be trying to infuse a high-energy enthusiasm, a calm laser focus, or a proactive predator-style mindset. Whatever your intended mindset, every movement and stance will either stoke the fire or extinguish it.

Any time the pressure is on, a natural part of your stress response includes tension and tightness throughout the body. You may not even be fully aware of those changes, but they will be feeding back information to your brain about how to feel as well as influencing how you move. Making a conscious choice about your mindset involves making a careful decision about your posture, movement, and breath.[3]

Takeaways

- Reframing is not lying to yourself or trying to convince yourself of something you don't believe. It is choosing to look at the situation from the perspective that is most helpful to you.

- Don't only choose how you frame the challenge ahead of you, but also consider how you perceive yourself going into it and what that means for how you will perform. Are you actively diving in with excitement for the challenge ahead, or will you skirt around the action, keeping your eyes on potential failures to avoid? Both options will lead to very different performances.

- The focus of your attention holds more power over your performance and your experience of it than you imagine. Immerse yourself in the task at hand. All future potential outcomes are merely a distraction from the focus required to be at your best.

- Use your words with precision and intention, respecting the force they exert on your emotion state and ability to focus. Choose them wisely.

- Shift your relationship with the stress response and the various sensations that we call anxiety. Welcome these sensations as your sign that your body is preparing a state of readiness for action. Use your breath to slow your heart rate if you need to and hold on tight to your chosen focus.

3

When it's hard to be with your feelings

CHAPTER 20

When you're overthinking everything

To bear trials with a calm mind robs misfortune of its strength and burden.

—Lucius Annaeus Seneca, *Hercules Oetaeus*

A letter from me to you

If you are overthinking everything right now, then you are undoubtedly well acquainted with the process of rushing into the worst-case scenario. So let's straight away tackle the worst-case scenario about overthinking. Many people who spend much of their lives worrying about things that might never happen imagine that this is just an unchangeable habit they will have to live with. But that is not the case. You do not have to be at the mercy of a current tendency to worry and the suffering it can cause.

The arrival of thoughts that predict the worst is as automatic as the intake of breath. But how we respond to them is different between individuals because it can be learned. Worrying about every little thing is not something you just have to put up with. It's about making those thoughts work for you and not against you.

A clear distinction between the times you feel terrified and the times you stride forward confidently is seen in whether you think you know what to do about a situation and whether you believe that your actions can have an effect. And this is the case when you catch yourself worrying about something. Once you have a template in mind and know how to respond, you can reap the value of the thoughts that have something to offer you and administer your own antidote to the suffering that results from spending too much time with the ones that do not.

Not only do you no longer need to live in the turmoil of holding on to thoughts that won't help. You also no longer need to add to your suffering with the anticipation of how much you know you will worry about everything that comes up.

It is true that you will face tomorrow with all the strength with which you faced today. But with the tools I am about to lay out for you, my intention is that you will face tomorrow with even more than you had at your disposal today. In fact, that is what happens every time you choose to actively stride forward in the face of fear and worry. How you respond to the worries of today creates the template in your mind for how you can respond to the worries of tomorrow. The responses that will come most naturally will be the ones you have put into action time and time again.

So let's shift from the defensive back foot, where you feel like the worry is dominating, to an offensive front foot, where you turn the story around and take action on this old pattern that makes life harder than it needs to be.

"How you respond to the worries of today creates the template in your mind for how you can respond to the worries of tomorrow. The responses that will come most naturally will be the ones you have put into action time and time again."

Real-time tools

While the tools in this section do work in real-time, the out-comes improve as you get better at applying them. That which feels laborious and hard work in the beginning will become second nature. As with everything, start with the easier shots by choosing smaller worries to tackle first so that you can get used to the process.

Understand the value of what your brain is doing

When it comes to your physical and psychological safety, you might say that your brain is the head of security. It takes clues from how your body is functioning and your senses to the outside world and presents to you ideas and predictions about what might be about to happen. Those predictions come in the form of feelings and thoughts. Sometimes those thoughts and feelings are useful to you and sometimes they're a distraction from other, more useful things. It is your job to decide what to do with them. You make the final decision on what ideas are most worth your continued attention and time.

Sometimes a worst-case scenario runs through your mind, and you immediately take action to prevent it from happening. That is you and your survival instinct working at your best together. But when it's not so immediate and it's not clear what action to take for the best outcome, there is a natural tendency to hold on to those predictions and churn them over in your mind, never fully coming to a conclusion or creating a plan but ramping up the fear that comes with it. We hold on to the thoughts that demand our attention, as if imagining negative outcomes over and over will lead us to a resolution somehow. But, while our brain producing these thoughts is of value, holding on to them without interrogating their value is unhelpful at best and leads to misery at worst. They begin to rob us of the strength to experience the vast array of more pleasant, meaningful, and positive emotions that are available to us in every given moment.

When it comes to tackling worry, we don't need to stop those worst-case scenario thoughts from arriving altogether. Instead, we need a clear and well-practiced process for what to do with them once they appear.

The key here is to hold in mind that your brain is doing its job of trying to keep you and your loved ones safe, and that it will never have all the facts necessary to get it right every time.

Don't be tempted to simply write yourself off as a worrier. Automatic thoughts are a normal human experience. They are not you. And you will not be subject to them once you practice choosing a new response.[1]

Review your overall stress

Most people focus on how overthinking causes them stress. But worrying is not the beginning of the stress response. This is one part of a broader cycle of stress that was (in most cases) set in motion some time before the worry even began. It's true that time spent worrying will increase your stress and feed that cycle. But it is also true that when stress is high, you are much more likely to think in this way.

When your body shows signs of stress, this will naturally cause you to be more vigilant and hypersensitive as your brain scans your environment for possible causes of that stress. Let's say, after a terrible night's sleep you have a few too many coffees the next morning to meet the demands at work. Then your loved one doesn't pick up the phone when you call, and your already stressed body leads your brain to be hypervigilant about this, and you start overthinking all the worst possible reasons that they haven't answered the phone. The already heightened stress made you more vulnerable to overthinking something that, on another day, you might not have given a second thought.

On top of that, given the level of stress, the brain starts to take a few cognitive shortcuts, and a thought bias appears, called fortune-telling. *I thought it, therefore it's true or at least definitely going to happen.* And that, in turn, ramps up the anxiety more and draws you to double down on those worst-case scenarios and play them out in your mind over and over.

You can see with this example that it makes less sense to focus on trying to stop worrying, and much more sense to review the wider context of your general stress levels. Go right back to the basics first. If you are not sleeping well, eating well, or exercising, then you will be more vulnerable to those worst-case scenario thoughts and the temptation to worry. If you are consuming too much caffeine or alcohol, or anything else that places stress on the body, then this will increase that hypervigilance too.

From there, review your stress in the wider context of your life. Whether it's relationships, work, or financial pressures, it is too easy to assume that those things are unrelated to the worry and anxiety that shows up in another area of your life, especially when the level of anxiety seems disproportionate and out of character. We have many different layers to our lives but just one stress response. If you notice that you've started over-thinking certain things that used to come easy, then it's especially helpful to take account of the bigger picture and how stressed you may have been before you even entered that situation.

Recognize and see the thoughts for what they are

It is possible to worry about something for hours before you even realize that you are doing it. The part that sounds easy enough but in fact takes some practice is noticing thoughts for what they are so that you can then choose what to do with them. Without seeing them for what they really are, we tend to accept them as factual and then give them all our attention.[2]

Here are three of the most common thought biases that you might notice when you're worrying.

1. **Catastrophizing.** No matter how unlikely it might be, the worst possible case scenario is the first thing that comes to mind. You then proceed to play it out in your mind like your own personal horror movie.

2. **Black-and-white thinking.** Also known as all-or-nothing thinking. This is when we think of things in extremes, ignoring the middle ground and all the shades of gray that might exist between those extremes.

3. **Fortune-telling.** This is our underlying assumption that, *I thought it, therefore it is true and must be likely to happen.* For example, convincing yourself that a job interview will go poorly, before it has even begun, based purely on the worries taken as factual.[3]

Once you spot any of these biases showing up, simply calling it out in your mind is the first step to getting a little distance from it and taking some of the power out of it. Sometimes that is enough to help you recognize that your thought is not a factual prediction of the future but only one possible way of looking at the situation. But if the thought needs a little more interrogating, then turn toward it with curiosity and ask some questions:

- Is it valid?
- Is it likely?
- Is it important?
- Is it changeable?
- Where is the bias in this idea or prediction?
- And most important, is this helpful to you?

Many people practice this process in a more formal and structured way, by writing down specific worries and then the answers to the questions. This is a great way of getting familiar with the process so that, in the moment when you most need to examine your thoughts, it comes more naturally and swiftly.

Take command of your attention and take action

Once you have interrogated those thoughts even just a little, you can see how the solution is less about not worrying at all and more about giving your valuable attention to the right things. To spend time worrying about something in a way that stands any chance of being helpful to you, it needs to be something that you have confirmed is true, important, and changeable.

Once you can see which of your worries are most worth your time, the antidote to all the destructive overthinking is to take action. If you can't start right now, then the second-best thing is to make a plan. Set out a clear map of your next steps in dealing with this. Preparing and taking one small first step toward tackling something has a monumentally different emotional outcome than sitting and waiting in fear.

Exercising your own sense of agency, even in small ways and in overwhelmingly inescapable situations, has the potential to transform the direction of your mental health. The person who concentrates their efforts on improving the moment, however slightly, will feel the effects that small actions can have on both the individual and the people around them, when they might otherwise feel paralyzed with worry.

Takeaways

- Don't be tempted to simply write yourself off as a worrier. We can learn to develop much more agency over the direction of our attention than you might think.

- Automatic thoughts that imagine the worst are not the problem. In fact, many of them hold value in keeping us safe. The main cause of suffering is the replaying of those little horror stories in your mind over and over again without ever turning that into constructive action to make things better.

- Overthinking will increase stress. But heightened stress will also increase your vulnerability to more worry thoughts and the temptation to fixate on them. If you find yourself overthinking things that normally don't bother you, this calls for a look at the bigger picture of your stress levels in the wider context of your life.

- When the brain senses threat, it takes shortcuts to work faster to keep you safe. Knowing that worry thoughts can be the product of a stress response means that they're often riddled with bias. Being able to spot that bias goes a long way to taking the power out of them.

- Asking questions like "Is it important?," "Is it likely?," "Is it changeable?," and "Is it helpful?" can act as a compass that helps us take command of where we place our attention.

CHAPTER 21

When fear shows up

Courage was not the absence of fear, but the triumph over it.

—Nelson Mandela

A letter from me to you

You are not responsible for fear showing up. You are responsible for the courage you cultivate to move through it. We are not at the mercy of fear. We are emotional shape-shifters and have been since the dawn of time. From the sharp focus of the samurai to the defiant war dance of the Māori, these are all acts of choosing a focus, choosing a mindset, choosing a response to even the biggest of fears. These communities were not fearless. They harnessed their fear in the most courageous way. That power to channel a laser-like attention and act with commanding composure is a choice that remains open to all of us.

The vigilance you feel is necessary. A sign you are ready. Activated and poised. By choosing to face your fear, you are cultivating strength that reaches deeper than you imagined it could. There is a fight in you of which you are barely scratching the surface. So breathe with ease. You are striding forward, not as prey, but as predator. Don't allow your focus to skip and jump between the shadows to be avoided. Look ahead, with an unfaltering focus on where you are headed.

Rehearse in your mind not all the possible horror stories but exactly what you intend to bring to the table. Ruminate on your chosen moves and how you intend to execute them, with courage as your driver.

The act of facing this will be the making of you: the crafting of your character that can come only from battling adversity. And by holding such unwavering determination, you will discover the power you have to cultivate the poise and composure that can channel the power of your bodily response into the action that you choose. The action that will leave you proud.

Get your chin up, throw your shoulders back, and start making those firm choices about how you plan to show up. Take absolute command of the story you tell yourself about what your fear means. It's here because you're doing something difficult. Just as a rocket's engines ignite and the roar of energy ripples through everything in range, that rush of fear through your body is something to welcome. It is the fuel that will get you through and out the other side.

You are about to bring your A game. And when you're finished, you will realize the power in you to choose how you show up and to use emotion to your advantage, the way it was meant to be used all along.

Real-time tools

Just a quick reminder that the tools I have included here are real-time tools that you can use to get you through difficult experiences as they happen. If you're trying to tackle a longer-term phobia or generalized anxiety, then a guide for how to do that is offered in the anxiety action plan included in the updated edition of my first book (see chapter 38 of *Why Has Nobody Told Me This Before?*).

But if you're facing something tough right now and you need to prime yourself with the right focus and mindset, these tools should get you started.

Fierce compassion

The only way to face fear with determination, defiance, and the commanding composure needed to engage with any challenge is to fully commit to having your own back. Do not be tempted to underestimate what this means. You cannot be perfunctory. You cannot talk to yourself in any way that could hold you back. You cannot be too hard or too soft on yourself. You cannot show contempt for yourself when you encounter setbacks. You have to know, above all else, that if the worst should happen, you will have your own back and do the absolute best by yourself. You will not turn on yourself the moment you show yourself to be fallible and human. When you commit to taking care of yourself as if you were both royalty and warrior, that approach will fuel your intended response instead of your retreat.

Fierce self-compassion means accessing more of the fight in your fight-or-flight response. It means driving forward through fear in order to do what you know is right for you or your loved ones. Doing what is hard now to forge a better future.

Attention is power

Stay vigilant about which thoughts, images, and feelings are helpful to you and which are not. We need to hold the unhelpful ones at arm's length, to get enough distance to see them for what they are, and to lock in on the thoughts and feelings that will get you through these tough moments.

Getting some distance from thoughts and feelings is sometimes called defusion. A quick way to do this in the moment is to write them down, giving you an instant bird's-eye view of what you're dealing with. It also helps to shift your language. Start each point with the words "I notice I'm having thoughts like . . ." or "I am noticing feelings of . . ." This creates a distinction between you and those experiences, helping you to recognize that you are not your thoughts or your feelings. They are your brain's summary of the meaning it is making from your body's reaction to the situation. When we can step back from them in this way, it is much easier to see how we can choose which perspectives to hold lightly and which ones to zoom in on.

This is not the same as repressing fear, which denies that it is present at all and often causes it to mutate and bubble up to the surface later when you have let your guard down and least expect it. You are not squashing all the fearful thoughts and feelings, or ignoring them. You are simply choosing to not let them drive.

Do not treat fear as the problem

Fear is not the problem. It is the signal to potential problems that might require your attention. When we see fear as something that is wrong with us, we judge it, fight it, and grasp at anything that will make it disappear. We spend all our efforts on shooting the messenger rather than working out what was being communicated and why.

Something else that many of us do is judge ourselves for feeling fear, as if the presence of fear means that we were somehow not brave or not coping. In reality, it might simply mean that you are facing something formidable. As the psychiatrist Carl Jung pointed out, "Where your fear is, there is your task."[1] If that is true, then of course you feel fear. Fear of the unknown, or fear of knowing exactly what is coming. Fear of the complexity of the problem and the weight of responsibility to get yourself and your loved ones through it. If fear is warranted, then let it be. When you stop fighting it, then it need not make your decisions for you. Take it with you, but base each step on who you intend to be in all of this, how you intend to show up.

By doing that, the things you face will not get easier, but you will become stronger, more courageous, valiant, and bold. Inherent in that process is a radical acceptance of life's challenges. If we do not feel entitled to a smooth ride, then we do not stew over the treacherous bumps and cracks in the road; we get to work on moving through them. And when you give with no expectation of anything in return, you discover the best of humanity along the way.

Reframe

The meaning you give to all of those physical sensations you're experiencing now will shape how you respond to and manage such fear in the future. Will it be your cue to step up and make yourself proud, or will you cower in fear of the fear itself? When I talk about reframing, this is not trying to dress up a painful emotion as something different or convince yourself that it is anything it's not. It is, in fact, coming back to reality.[2]

The more science reveals about how emotions are created, the more we come to understand that we each have more power to cultivate our experience and control our approach than we were ever taught to believe.

Your brain is constantly telling itself a story about what is going on in your body in relation to the world outside and using memories of what has happened in the past to help predict what is coming next and how you should react.[3] Your feelings are a part of the expression of the summary it comes up with. As you make your way through changing scenarios, your emotions are essentially guesswork. You can choose what you do with those guesses. They can be a sign that you are in a tough situation, doing hard things. Or they can be a sign of any number of other things, like a lack of sleep, a new and unpredictable situation, a lack of skills to meet a big demand, exhaustion, limiting beliefs. The list goes on. But the powerful part you can play is by priming your brain to focus on particular aspects and choose actions that feed the emotional response you need to get you through.

If you felt like a rabbit in the headlights before, perhaps my letter to you at the beginning of this chapter shifted that image,

"Fear is
the core
ingredient
of courage."

just by transforming the language. You don't have to go with that description if it doesn't quite fit you or your situation. The key is to use your words with precision and the intention to do the best by yourself through whatever you are facing.

At the very least, remember that fear is the core ingredient of courage and a cue to engage in the fight ahead. Fear is also temporary, so use it while you have it. We can endure hard things more readily and make use of our tools more efficiently when we know the tricky times won't last forever.

Takeaways

- You are not responsible for fear showing up. You are responsible for the courage you now cultivate to move through it.

- The vigilance you feel is necessary. A sign you are ready. Activated and poised. By choosing to face this, you are cultivating strength that reaches deeper than you imagined it could.

- Rehearse in your mind not all the possible horror stories but exactly what you intend to bring to the table. Ruminate on your chosen moves and how you intend to execute them, with courage as your driver.

- The only way to face fear with determination, defiance, and the commanding composure needed to engage in the challenge is to fully commit to having your own back.

- Stay vigilant about which thoughts, images, and feelings are helpful to you and which are not. We need to hold the unhelpful ones at arm's length, to get enough distance to see them for what they are, and to lock in on the thoughts and feelings that will get you through these tough moments.

- Do not be tempted to see fear as anything other than the messenger. When we see it as a fault within ourselves, we search for ways to make it all disappear. Do not judge it or fight it. Feeling fear does not mean something is wrong with you. It does not mean you are not brave or not coping. It might simply mean that you are facing something tough.

CHAPTER 22

When grief overwhelms you

The pain of grief is just as much a part of life as the joy of love; it is, perhaps, the price we pay for love, the cost of commitment.

—Dr. Colin Murray Parkes

A letter from me to you

I write this to you with no anticipation of what you are feeling or the depth of your pain. But I imagine it goes deeper than you or I have the words to describe. I am not about to tell you what to feel or how to think. Whatever you feel right now, go ahead and feel it.

Grief is not just one emotion. It is a thread that runs through all of them. Every reminder brings forth the pain that we have no idea how to navigate. But every memory also holds the love, the laughter, the comfort, and the calm we felt when the person we are grieving for was here. How is it possible to feel the warmth of their presence within those memories alongside such agony for their absence? How is it possible to experience the lightness of being in a small moment of distraction? A pocket of time when life could almost be as it was before. Only to have reality thump you in the chest and plunge you back into the darkness of deep, agonizing pain.

These natural intervals are often followed by feelings of guilt for having had a moment without pain. How dare I forget, even for three seconds? And if that person faced a long illness or decline, the relief we feel that their suffering has ended becomes entangled with the yearning for their return.

These emotions collide, all seeming to clash and contradict each other, each one making the other hard to swallow. It's difficult to make sense of any of it.

If grief really is the price we pay for love, then bring it on. Because no amount of pain would ever make us want to change the fact that our person had existed, that we had the chance to love them.

So bring all your strength to bear on this pain. Allow it to come forth in all its wretchedness and to take its natural course. We can grieve yet feel gratitude for the connection we had, and continue that connection, albeit in a new way that we didn't choose.

The imprint your person left in your mind and your body still exists. They remain with you, connected in this new way. Not only in the memories you keep, but in everything they ever made you feel, in all the rituals you shared: the knowing looks, the private jokes, the shared understanding, and the person you became by knowing them.

Your body remembers what it feels like to be next to them, to be talking to them, to listen to them. The challenge of grief is not to deny or squash that but to bring it to the surface when you so desire. This doesn't mean living in denial that they are gone, but learning to cherish and nurture that imprint and to honor the mark they left in your world.

Real-time tools

There's no room for casual advice when it comes to grief, so the things listed here are based on what we know from the literature, from the people who have found ways through, and from the professionals who supported them along the way.

Ditch the expectations

There is no end point to grief, and why should there be? The experience and characteristics of it may change over time, and that's okay. You may get more freedom to choose when to step into the pain and when to step out, when to connect with your memories and when to engage with life as it is now.

Don't feel guilty about grieving. It is entirely necessary. Give yourself time to adjust to such a life-altering loss.

Grief is often chaotic and unpredictable. That is not a reflection of any measure of coping. It is the very nature of grief. Put a hand to your heart, feel the warmth, and remind yourself that this is both natural and terribly difficult. The last thing you need in these moments is another layer of pain added by some arduous standards you are supposed to observe in how you grieve.

Experiencing depression symptoms after a bereavement is not unusual or indeed pathological in any way, but be sure to do the things that will help during that period. Let the people in your life comfort and support you, spend time outdoors, move your body every day, and make time for deep rest.

Let it rain, but take an umbrella

As the grief psychotherapist Julia Samuel puts it, "Pain is the agent of change."[1] Allowing yourself to spend time feeling whatever comes up will help you find a way to adjust to this new reality. But you don't have to spend every minute of every day absorbed in the pain. It's okay to shield yourself for a while with the distractions of life. You will find small things that offer temporary comfort or distraction and some rest from the physical and emotional exhaustion of grief.

But not all distractions are equal, and it is important that when you are at your most vulnerable, you steer clear of things that offer to numb the pain at a cost to your health or ability to function later. Alcohol and drugs are the obvious ones, but the often overlooked and more subtle ways we numb include overworking and overfunctioning in order to avoid the reminders and the pain they bring. While it is a positive thing to return to meaningful work, it can become compulsive when used as an avoidance strategy. Stillness brings more grief, so taking breaks becomes impossible, until burnout strikes and your body forces rest upon you. It pays to use distractions wisely and to recognize that some time spent allowing those feelings to be felt is the path to healthy adjustment.

Don't turn your pain on the ones who remain

Whether it's an expression of the pain or an avoidance of it, turning on one another can only make a tragic situation worse for everybody. Let others hold you steady when you feel broken—and hold them in return. In the face of loss, it is the love for and connection with the people in our lives that carries us through.

Families and friends who pull together and support one another prevent the isolation that often befalls us after a bereavement. No one can do the work of grieving for you, but they can walk through it with you, ensuring that you don't do it alone.

Stirring up resentment in others will only damage the connections you have to the people you have left. Don't let this experience make you hateful or bitter.

Don't turn the pain on yourself

We feel guilty when grief hits, and guilty when it doesn't, guilty for what we did, and guilty for what we didn't do. Guilt seems to pop up everywhere, and inherent in all of it is often affording ourselves more agency than we ever truly had.

We wrestle with all the combinations of "what if" stories, fantasizing about the different choices we could or should have made, testing out new versions of the story in our minds, trying out different endings. Or we torture ourselves with the illusion that it is all our fault.

This is all a part of the yearning for the person who is now gone and the bargaining we try to do with this new reality that we didn't want. It is a natural part of that process. But where you can, let that guilt go free and come back to the present moment. Turning your pain on yourself will not make the past better, but it will make the future worse.

Acknowledge and express

The relationship with your loved one doesn't end. It changes. So speaking of them when they come to mind and acknowledging when their absence is felt becomes a part of the adjustment process for everyone. This can be more difficult when everything is raw and when we don't want to make others feel upset on special occasions. But this can also be a source of continued connection. The lighting of a candle at Christmas dinner, the making of their favorite meal on their birthday, a toast to the one we all miss so deeply. These small acknowledgments help us not only to express the pain of their absence but also to connect with one another in our grief. When talking doesn't feel like an option, expression of grief can be more private. Writing in a journal, or a favorite creative endeavor, can help to release what we cannot speak.

If you try to block it out and deny the pain that you and your loved ones are feeling, you diminish your capacity to connect with one another. Everybody is hurting, but everyone is afraid to show up with that pain. Your mask meets mine, and we exchange nothing but pleasantries, both feeling more lonely than we did before but unable to speak the unspeakable. In the same respect, you cannot selectively numb emotions. When you numb the painful ones, you also numb the positive ones. You cannot stop to enjoy all the things that once brought you pleasure for fear of the pain showing up. This is why allowing yourself to feel and express the sorrow enables you to both grieve your loved one and reengage in life as it is today, with moments in which you can be truly present.

Connect

Quite possibly the most important point to share about grief is that continued connection to both the loved one who is gone and the loved ones who remain is the guiding light to keep in your view.

"Turning your pain on yourself will not make the past better, but it will make the future worse."

It is possible to find ways to connect and feel close to them without their physical presence. When we yearn for their presence, we can meet that with rituals, shrines, or special places that allow you to feel that closeness. A single item that held meaning between you can remain in your pocket for moments you most need it.

Alongside this, focus your energy on maintaining and nurturing connections with the people in your life. If there's one thing you take from this chapter, let it be this: Go toward the people in your life and do the things that make this terrible situation a little less awful for each of you. Be in it together. The urges to withdraw will be strong at times, but don't allow that to isolate you for too long.

Movement changes your brain chemistry

When the world as you knew it is pulled from beneath you and everything has changed, your body will be in fight-or-flight mode much of the time as you recall what has happened and face a different future to the one you had imagined. Alongside that, deep sadness and emptiness weigh down on attempts to engage in everyday life.

Of the people I have worked with over the years who have experienced bereavement, many of them say that exercise was instrumental in their capacity to nurture their own mental health in the face of their grief. The research backs this up, and we know that any form of movement that increases your heart rate and demands that you breathe more deeply and use your muscles has a considerable impact on your brain chemistry that acts as a springboard for mental health.[2] Within a few minutes of exercise you experience a boost of adrenaline and dopamine that gives you more energy and counters the fatigue that so often accompanies grief. After twenty minutes a mix of endorphins and endocannabinoids has been shown to enhance our capacity for optimism, pleasure, and connection with others. In grief all three of those need as much help as they can get.

Whatever your choice of movement, if you do it alongside other people, your brain senses that connection and you can benefit from an enhanced sense of belonging and trust, and generally feel less alone. There is no pressure to sign up for anything drastic and overwhelming when you may have barely left the house in weeks. Steps that are small, manageable, and potentially enjoyable are much more likely to be sustained and benefited from in the long-term. So aim to increase movement in the way that suits you best.

Takeaways

- Whatever you feel, go ahead and feel it. Drop any expectations about what you should feel and for how long.

- It is okay to create space between the big emotions with distractions that interrupt the pain, even just for a little while.

- Don't give in to temptation to turn the pain on yourself or the people who love you. This can be an expression of the pain or an avoidance of it, but is guaranteed to turn an already awful situation into an unbearable one.

- Grief is not just an experience of the mind but also the body. Exercise in one form or another can be pivotal in rebuilding and reinforcing mental health through a bereavement. This doesn't have to be formal exercise routines. It could be as simple as walks in nature or a gentle swim with a friend.

- Connection is the key when it comes to grief. There will undoubtedly be urges to withdraw, but be careful not to isolate yourself for too long. Support and let yourself be supported by the people in your life.

- It is also okay to find small ways to feel connected to the person you're grieving for, perhaps via special objects that hold memories or places you can go to feel closer to them.

CHAPTER 23

When everything feels pointless

Even the darkest night will end and the sun will rise.

—Victor Hugo, *Les Misérables*

A letter from me to you

When you take too many heavy hits in quick succession and for a while all your efforts feel in vain, you might start to question what it's all for. Everything starts to feel pointless. The most basic of tasks begins to feel like more trouble than it's worth. We lose our memory of the joy that can be found in effort and question the point of every act before we commit to it.

This is among the most human of experiences and yet a dangerous place to be. Depression grows fast in a mind that loses a sense of purpose.[1] But you are not stuck here. This is something you can change. The feeling that everything is pointless is not a reflection of a life with no value. It is a signal for you to reevaluate and get to work. Do not wait for the meaning of life to be presented to you. It reveals itself in your actions and efforts and how you respond to each challenge that you face. Even this dark time that you're going through, questioning the point of every-thing, has a purpose. You've caught a glimpse of how bleak it gets and the emptiness from being temporarily blinded to the meaning in life. So your new mission, your new purpose, is to find your way back, to find your way out of that gloom until you have a better view of the bigger picture once again. In the process you will uncover strength that you never had the chance to witness before, and in better times you'll feel unstoppable in comparison to the adversity you fought through.

To make your suffering worthwhile is very much the point. Life is hard and full of effort. But when we direct that effort toward contribution beyond ourselves, we are living in line with human nature. Watch anyone come alive when they are given the chance to make their mark and bring something of value to the people in their life. As you do that, you'll see the value in everything you do. But the moving must come first. If you don't start moving, depression will engulf you. When everything feels pointless, you must create the role for yourself that is worth living for. If you are willing to take charge of where you are going, this next chapter will be your becoming.

To begin, you must trust that working on this will bring you to somewhere better than here. Sometimes when you feel like you're sinking, you lose your sense of everything glorious that awaits you on the surface. You feel the immense pressure that makes any effort hard work. When your mind falls into deep water like this and confusion reigns, the only thing to do is hold on and start kick-ing like hell. Start moving against the resistance that's pushing you down. Not being able to envisage that better future just yet only tells us about the limitations of our imagination.

You see, being here is not a meaningless burden. It is a chance, an opportunity to step up for a world with no end of need that you could ease. Grasp the responsibility of becoming everything you can possibly be so that you can leave things a little better than you found them.

Real-time tools

If you have been plagued for some time with the feeling that everything is pointless, then don't gloss over these tools, turn each one into a concrete plan of action. You have a fight on your hands, and reading this book alone will not turn it all around. Taking action will do that. As somebody who has worked with many people who have found themselves in this living hell that is helplessness and hopelessness, I know that you need to crack down on that rumination right now. You don't need to block out those thoughts. But turn to face forward. By this I mean, accept that this feeling is here now, but never ever assume that just because you cannot find a sense of meaning at this moment, that there is no meaning to be found.

One small thing
When you tell yourself that nothing you do can ever make a difference, that narrative is guaranteed to bring you down. Nobody thrives on that belief, but many perish. The stakes are high enough that it's worth questioning just how true this thought is. And the only way to find out the answer is to try. Go and do something helpful, something worthwhile, and see if you can prove that thought wrong. See if you can do one small thing to

improve the moment. What is one thing you are doing right now that is making this moment worse for you? Quite possibly, questioning whether everything is pointless is one of those things. So let's get to work finding something that feels more meaningful than this rumination. You're not trying to convince yourself of anything you don't believe yet. You're simply investigating, searching for the truth.

It's okay if you don't know where to start. Nobody does. Just begin. Find the nearest thing that you could apply yourself to and go do it. Start so small that it almost feels laughable. Then you cannot convince yourself that it's not possible. There is no need to look too far ahead. Stay in the moment. Once that one small thing is done, then you have success under your belt: a sign that you have more to offer than ruminating on life. So one small thing can lead to the next and the next, and you'll reap the benefits as you go.

Contribute

Nothing opens our eyes to meaning more than our most human instincts to connect with people around us and contribute to their efforts for one another. I can almost guarantee that, if you are questioning the point of everything, you feel disconnected from the people in your life or that the contribution you're making to those humans does not sit in line with your values.

When you feel detached and set apart from others, and when you feel like you are not making any recognizable difference to their lives, you start to feel invisible. But you are more connected than you think. Every single person who crosses your path is affected by you. They are nourished by your efforts to improve the moment, or they miss out when you decide not to.

They unknowingly suffer the consequences when you do not look after yourself enough to bring your strengths to the world.

The perfect counterweight to all the rumination about feeling insignificant is to look outward and see if you can make something better for somebody else. There is no shortage of need out there. Take on even the smallest of responsibilities to help someone else in whatever way you can. When you discover that you can contribute and ease the suffering of others in any small way, when you discover that you can leave people and places in a slightly better state than when you arrived, it moves the dial in a way that rumination never will. Your drive is ignited by your contribution. What matters is not how big and bold your contribution is but that it is a positive one.

When everything feels pointless to you, your mind will be looking for reasons not to try. *It won't work, nothing will change how I feel, nothing I do matters.* Giving those thoughts airtime will take you down only one path. That path is dark and lonely, and leads to a life of misery and despair. So when your mind offers up the thought that this small contribution you are about to make is worthless and a waste of time, hold that thought lightly and resolve to test it out for yourself.

Move to lift your mood

When you are feeling hopeless or helpless about life, this is not the time to be contemplating unanswerable questions. Your focus must be on placing your attention on the things that make your life better and thereby shifting your state. Without a doubt, one of the most potent ways to shift your state is to move your body.[2] It doesn't matter if you are walking, swimming, climbing a tree, cleaning your house: it all counts. Do something physical every day. If you can combine that with time spent outside or connecting with other people, then you get the added benefits. Try engaging in movement that simply feels like play, doing something active for no other reason than you might enjoy it. Also make time for movement in the form of a job or project that will give you visible results. Whether it's scrubbing the bathroom, mowing the lawn, or tidying up, the completion of these things marks progress and builds momentum, while the physical effort will help to lift your mood and shift you out of rumination.

If your thoughts of everything feeling pointless are in the context of depression, and especially if you are socially isolated, then seeking professional support is highly recommended if you have access to this.

Connect for perspective

Do not be alone in your suffering. Our connections with the people in our lives help give meaning to things. Spending time with others will naturally help to shift perspectives that can become warped from isolation. Sharing what you have been going through with someone you trust can begin to normalize those feelings and at the same time let you see past them toward a brighter future. Connecting with the people you care about will open your eyes to the needs that surround you and how others could benefit from your help. Everyone is dealing with problems, and your friends and loved ones will be grateful to have you there beside them as they work through their own challenges.

"What matters is not how big and bold your contribution is but that it is a positive one."

If you are feeling isolated from others and terrified at the thought of reaching out to anyone, there are still options available to you. Depending on where you are in the world and what's available, you might be able to reach out to charities or support services, or your doctor may be able to point you in the right direction. It is also possible to connect with people in your community in small ways and at your own pace. Perhaps you strike up a conversation with the person you see at the bus stop every day or at the checkout of your local shop. Or a simple hello to a neighbor in the street. These short but regular interactions can be a great way to build your confidence by practicing, if you are feeling isolated.

Reevaluate

Once you have shifted your mood and emotion state with these tasks and you have committed to a more positive routine, take some time to reassess things. You're likely to be in a better position now to look clearly at what made you vulnerable to feeling that way. Consider all the things that contributed to your low mood over time, including both the context of your life and the choices you were making. Reflecting in this way can give you a sense of direction. There might be small changes to make, but there also might be some bigger ones. Set some short-term goals and some bigger, longer-term ones that help point the way. You can use the "Anticipate challenges ahead" exercise in the appendix (see page 305) to make sure that the goals you set are based on what matters most to you at this point in your life.

Only you can make those calls for yourself, so make sure you do this task when you can think clearly and feel strongly that you want to start doing the best by yourself.

Takeaways

- Feeling that life is pointless is among the most human of experiences yet a dangerous place to be. Depression grows fast in a mind that loses a sense of purpose. But you are not stuck here. This is something you can change.

- The feeling that everything is pointless is not a reflection of a life with no value. It is a signal for you to re-evaluate and get to work. Do not wait for the meaning of life to be presented to you. It reveals itself in your actions and efforts and how you respond to each challenge that you face.

- To make your suffering worthwhile is very much the point. Life is hard and full of effort. But when we direct that effort toward contribution beyond ourselves, we are living in line with human nature. Watch anyone come alive when they're given the chance to make their mark and bring something of value to the people in their life.

- Accept that this feeling is here now, but never ever assume that just because you cannot find meaning today, that there is no meaning to be found.

- Do not be alone in your suffering. It is our connections with the people in our lives that gives meaning to things. Spending time with others will naturally help to shift perspectives that can become warped from isolation.

- Nothing opens our eyes to meaning more than our most human instincts to connect with other people and contribute to their efforts for one another.

CHAPTER 24

When you feel like an imposter

I am not a writer. I've been fooling myself and other people.

—John Steinbeck, *Working Days*

A letter from me to you

If you find yourself in a situation that demands a lot from you and you're not sure if you can live up to that, then this is better news than you might think. Feeling like an imposter is something we all go through when we are stepping up and putting ourselves to the test so that we can progress and improve. In those environments we surround ourselves with people we can learn from and immediately feel humbled and then intimidated by how smart and competent they seem to be. At this point it's almost a reflex to start judging yourself as unworthy of your place in the room. You disregard the potential seen by the people who put you there. On top of that, you bring with you an intimate knowledge of your every flaw and inadequacy along with total ignorance of everyone else's.

The more you compare your beginner status with their seasoned mastery, the more you believe that you will never be as talented or as successful as them. It's pure chance that you're even here. So how on earth do you expect to live up to this challenge? You just know the first setback you encounter will be seen in your mind as evidence that you are not good enough and never will be.

A good deal of the pain in all this is the illusion that we are alone in these feelings. No one else is this ridiculous. When we are stepping into what feels like a battleground, with unyielding scrutiny and the prospect of humiliation, we get the sense that we feel this way because we are surpassing our own capacity, punching above our weight. We don't imagine for a moment that every other human who has passed through this particular arena felt the same, or that they, too, started at the bottom and worked their way up burdened by all the usual human flaws.

It's too easy in these moments to lose all sense of how you want to show up in the world. You tighten your grip on dignity to avoid humiliation, and the side effect is often regret. The urge to make excuses, turn your back on the challenge, or buy into the promises of perfectionism will all be strong. But you are not a helpless passenger on this journey. You are the pilot. You could have chosen to step back, to avoid this. But you didn't. That is something to be proud of.

Of course fear is present. It is present every time we see that we could be more than what we are today. Every time we get the chance to try to exceed what we thought our limits were. And when that fear temporarily blurs your vision, like tears filling the eyes, you lose sight of the fact that your hands are on the controls, but it's just a really tough mission.

Despite that, I'm not about to tell you that all those "I'm not good enough" thoughts are pathological and untrue. At the beginning of most ventures, you probably won't be good enough. But those thoughts don't have to be threatening if you see the power you have to improve with effort. They can be an indication of where to channel your learning next. That mindset is going to drive you forward. It's okay not to be good enough for now because you are going to make sure it's not permanent.

Fear and self-doubt become the resistance to push against, not a reason to stop. In fact, it's the reason you're here. When you feel no resistance, you're standing still, treading water. Pushing against something is the sign that you're working hard and real progress is about to happen.

But what if you fail? What if you completely humiliate yourself? Well, if you do, then you will learn the painful lesson that you can in fact survive failure and haul yourself back up. You will also learn that most of the horror stories playing out in your mind don't come true.

Real-time tools

It is important to remember that feeling like an imposter is a normal part of human existence. No one gets to skip it. In fact, many of the high-status individuals you perceive as unstoppable and flawless have probably felt it the most. They had to, in order to get to where they are.

The feeling becomes a problem only when you're unwilling to accept it, unwilling to act in its presence. The following tools are not aimed at making that feeling disappear. That will happen by itself when you drive forward and progress. The aim is to arm you with everything you need to hold that feeling lightly while you do what it takes to go beyond what you thought were your limits.

Spot the bias

Your emotions are a reflection of your brain's attempt to make sense of things. When you feel vulnerable or stressed, your thoughts come up with a narrative to match that feeling. Don't let imposter thoughts—thoughts that you are a fraud, undeserving of your seat at the table, or predictions that someone will expose you as inadequate and humiliate you—go unchecked. These are the thoughts that will keep that imposter feeling alive and magnify the fear. With some practice, it gets easier to spot the bias and absurdity in such ideas.

When you feel like an imposter, notice that your thoughts tend to focus on your apparent incompetence, and in particular on how other people are judging that incompetence. This is a great time to remind yourself of the spotlight effect.[1] All humans overestimate the amount to which other people are judging them negatively. In fact, in the research on this, the only time that people tend to make an accurate estimate is when they are onstage performing. Understanding that these phenomena exist can become helpful in real life, just by bringing them to mind. Remember that this is something we do as humans, that might lead us to feel more self-conscious than we need to be. Unless you're performing onstage or being tested, most people are not judging you as much as you tell yourself they are. This phenomenon need not be fixated on in order to be overcome. Simply acknowledge it so that you can hold those spotlight thoughts a little more lightly.

Another common tendency is to personalize. You attribute all your mistakes in the learning process to your apparently permanent deficiencies. You consider mistakes made by other people more fairly in the context of all the demanding hurdles they faced along the way. The former leads to shame and the urge to give up; however, extending the latter to yourself invites learning and progress. When you notice a few personalizing thoughts crop up, call out the bias and offer up a counterweight that is a tad more realistic.

Honesty

When you feel like a fraud, the most important thing you can do is to not confirm that fear with your behavior. The fear will tell you to cover up your imperfections and lie about your competencies, to focus on making it look like you can keep up. Don't be tempted to do this. If you are honest about your beginner status and your willingness to learn and contribute as much as you can along the way, few people will judge you for that. In fact, they are likely to trust and respect you more. Those with more experience will tend to judge only those who deny their shortcomings and claim to know more than they do. Most people do not judge someone who is open and honest about their early stage of development, someone willing to ask questions.

Be of service and be a self-declared work in progress. Being a lifelong learner means you will often feel slightly out of your depth. The feeling reflects how you are living, not a measure of your adequacy.

"Be a
self-declared
work in
progress."

Self-respect over self-esteem

Much of the advice offered online around imposter syndrome assumes that what is needed is an increase in self-esteem. But this is
not a helpful focus. It suggests that your view of yourself as a humble and possibly vulnerable beginner is wrong, and that as long as
you feel better about yourself, then the world will believe the same.

But self-esteem is not necessarily the path to happiness that
has been suggested over the years.[2] It can correlate with narcissism, anger, aggression, and bullying as well as values such as ma-
terialism and vanity—valuing money and fame over family and
community.

An inflated view of the self is not helpful to you and won't be
very pleasant for the people you love. An accurate and fair estimation of the self, treated with the same respect you would offer to
anyone you wanted the best for, is much more valuable to you. This
means taking care to hold yourself as a person of value in your right
to exist just like everyone else, and accepting yourself as a work in
progress, followed by an outward focus on the value of hard work
with the aim of contributing to others. You accept that you are human just like everyone else, with a lot to learn along the way. At
the same time, you commit to learning more and doing better so
that you can make a valuable contribution to the world.[3]

Unfair comparisons

Don't compare your beginning to their middle. When you see
others who are further along on their journey to achieve success,
switch from judgmental comparison to curious inspiration. How
did they get here? What can you learn from them?

If you judge everyone in the room to be smarter or more

competent than you, that makes you the luckiest person in the room. That means you have the best chance to make the most progress. Don't enter the room just to compete. See the bigger picture of your life. Come into the room to absorb and take all the learning that you can while contributing as much value as possible along the way.

Takeaways

- When you are stepping up to a new challenge, feeling like an imposter is a natural part of that process because it will highlight what you are yet to learn and accomplish.

- Watch out for emotional reasoning here. Feeling like a fraud does not mean that you are one. You get to choose to be honest about your status as a beginner and openly commit to simultaneously learning and contributing value along the way.

- Rather than compare yourself to those who are further along in their journey, look to them as sources of inspiration and learning. If you feel like the most inexperienced one in the room, then you have the biggest opportunity for growth. This is a great situation, not a bad one.

- You do not always have to think highly of yourself. You benefit most from thinking honestly and respectfully about yourself and wanting the absolute best for yourself in the future. Beyond that, shift your focus outward and put your efforts into making worthwhile contributions. Constantly evaluating yourself is not good for your mental health.

CHAPTER 25

When you have done something you regret

On no account brood over your wrongdoing. Rolling in the muck is not the best way of getting clean.

—Aldous Huxley, *Brave New World*

A letter from me to you

If you look back and feel the pain of regret over actions that don't reflect how you want to live your life, welcome to being human. The hard truth is that we learn as much about the kind of person we want to be by getting things wrong as we do from getting them right. Feelings of guilt, regret, and remorse are your signal that there is learning to be done.

But you get stuck if you allow the expectation that you should have known back then what you know now, that you should have known the lesson before you learned it. Or indulging in the fantasy that you should have been perfect from day one to be acceptable and loveable, that mistakes are somehow proof that you are not worthy after all. We can even put the world itself on a pedestal, especially if we grew up with a view of life as perfect as long as we are getting things right.

The realization that the world and life within it is fraught with costs to every gain is a painful one. Our assumption that, as long as we get things right, everything will be okay and we'll have a life with no regrets turns out to be wrong. There is a cost to every choice, even the right ones. Some of those costs you can live with, others plague you for years after.

I do not write to you with the intention of talking you out of your regret. Your regret is not the problem. But your reaction to it might be. Emotions are a best guess about what is going on, so your first position should be to ask yourself if this feeling is warranted. If you have a tendency to constantly second-guess yourself and ruminate on everything that's wrong with the decisions you make, then regret might well be a symptom of that destructive pattern. If that's the case, this chapter on feeling guilty over everything you do might be for you. But if you genuinely made a misstep and find yourself remorseful about it, then those feelings can be a force for good if you are brave enough to examine them.

There are some things only adversity can teach you.[1] So let it do that. Be willing to look at the thing you least want to look at. Not as a source of self-loathing, but as a source of wisdom.

In life, finding the right path is a process that unfolds as much through discovering the dead ends as encountering new pathways. None of us start out in life dreaming of all the things we will get wrong, but taking wrong turns plays a role in finding the right ones. If you see each of those dead ends as a lesson learned, you unfold the map in your mind that shows the direction to take next. Rather than regret being a slippery slope into hopelessness, you will instead turn on your heel and keep moving.

You have the power to turn regret into the beginnings of progress, but for that to happen you must resist the temptation to see your mistakes as any indication of your worthiness. Without guilt to listen to, you could have become someone very different from the person you are aiming for now. Give the feeling its due, and recognize its value. Guilt has an incredible ability to press pause on downward spirals.[2] Contrary to the misconception that listening to guilt is weakening, in reality it demands a depth of courage to acknowledge when you might be heading in the wrong direction, away from the type of person you want to be. In this way guilt is just another emotion offering a signal that perhaps not all is well, in particular, where living in line with our values is concerned.

Real-time tools

Some people squash feelings of regret or guilt, refusing to acknowledge them. Others spend years being consumed by them. Somewhere in between those two extremes is a place where you get to turn toward them with curiosity, use what is helpful, and let go of what is not. Doing that is not always easy. It takes courage and self-discipline to look at where you've gone wrong without turning on yourself in a destructive way. This subject alone could fill many books, but here are a couple of crucial tools to get you started.

"There are some things only adversity can teach you."

Halt the rumination

We all do things that bring up guilt or shame and humiliation at times. Those who follow that up with rumination—thinking over and over about the things they feel most ashamed of—will corrode their own sense of self-worth and struggle to move on. When we are steeped in shame, we cannot think clearly, let alone learn. When we do this, we become so consumed in this self-punishing process that it prevents us from doing the things that could repair the damage, make amends, or take what we've learned to create a more positive future.

As you churn over and over the most painful and destructive thoughts about what happened, you are doing the opposite of helping yourself. All of this time spent wrestling with the fact that you got something wrong is an avoidance of simply listening to the sensation and acting on it in the way that it is asking to be resolved. If you made a mistake and then repaired the rupture that was caused in your relationship, you can reap the lessons and leave the guilt behind. Rumination gets us stuck in a loop of wishing we could change the past. But if we attend to the present, we can improve the future. Everything we so spectacularly got wrong becomes a catalyst for worthwhile change.

When you recognize that you are ruminating, call a stop to it straight away. You can either try to shift into a more productive thought process and consider how you might make things better, or (if you are not ready for that yet) you can do something active that demands your attention in order to bring yourself back into the present.

This is mindfulness in action when you most need it. Starting some kind of mindfulness practice will help you notice and stop

271

rumination more easily in the future. But if you need to stop rumination now, use any activity that you can easily absorb yourself in to break the rumination cycle.

Take action to repair

If you are sure that your feeling of guilt is warranted and proportionate to the situation, then don't try to convince yourself out of it, ignore it, or numb it. Moving on from guilt requires new action in the direction you need to be going. Such actions demonstrate that you can be fallible yet acceptable: these actions may deeply repair a torn relationship or make new, trusting ones.

One of the trip wires when it comes to resolving guilt, or at least when the damage caused was not too big for an apology to bridge the void between you and the other person, is our struggle with apologizing and our lack of ability to do it effectively. Apology is necessary but not always sufficient to mend a rupture in a relationship. If you try to rebuild a relationship without it, you are building on shaky ground, but an apology that simply marks a return to the way things were is a foundation left bare. While an apology that truly repairs a relationship starts with "I'm sorry," it must be followed by a clear shift in behavior that proves to the person that you intend to do things differently from this point on.

But if we get the initial apology wrong or it comes across as insincere, the other person is likely to be suspicious and unconvinced of any change in behavior, which can lead to further ruptures. With that in mind, let's have a quick look at what makes a great apology.

Researchers have identified six components that contribute to the most effective apology.

1. Naming your regret for what happened

Being clear about what happened and that you genuinely feel regret takes the simple "I'm sorry" to a new level. There's often disagreement about the way something happened and who was to blame. But taking radical responsibility for one's own behavior (even in murky waters in which you felt justified at the time) is a stamp of quality on a decent apology. The tendency is often to defend our mistake or wrongdoing by blaming the other person or the circumstances in some way. It takes some guts to show accountability for your actions regardless of the factors that may have influenced you at the time. And rather than making you seem weak, on the contrary this displays decency and courage and builds greater trust that you don't just move where the wind blows you. The other person needs to know that circumstance will not make this likely to happen again. A tough order to get right, but incredibly powerful.

2. Saying the words "I'm sorry"

Don't skirt around this one. It does not lessen you in any way to say I'm sorry when you have wronged another person. But it will move the needle on your attempts to repair and reconnect with the people you love when you've made a mistake or wronged them in some way. Even with all the other details in this list, it means a great deal to many people to hear the words.

3. Sincerely asking for forgiveness

One can request forgiveness from another only in the context of taking full responsibility for the wrongdoing and the impact it had. Without that accountability, it sounds much more like asking to be let off the hook. This is a highly uncomfortable thing to do and undoubtedly a big reason that so many of us find it so hard to do. If the harm caused to the other person was beyond the scope of the everyday, then it might feel more appropriate to instead state that you understand forgiveness is a process that takes time and that your apology is sincere whether forgiveness is possible or not.

4. Validating the feelings of the other person

We naturally shy away from naming the hurt we have caused another person for fear that we will bring it back to the surface and trigger another shouting match. But showing that you have some level of understanding about how they might feel and that you care about that, in fact, tends to have the opposite effect. Anger is often present when we don't feel heard. Voicing an acknowledgment of the potential emotional consequences of your mistake therefore goes a long way to bringing down the intensity of any anger. Feeling seen by another person also does wonders for reconnection and beginning to rebuild trust because it's a rationale for apology that feels most likely to lead to genuine change. If you sense that someone is apologizing because they hate the idea that they hurt you, this feels very different from an apology just to end the discussion or to gain something from you.

Whether you agree with their perception of things or not, demonstrating that you can understand how they felt and that you can see the situation from their perspective is key. You can then express your own remorse for that hurt and that you care deeply if they're not okay.

5. Offering atonement

If there was clear unfairness in what happened, it might be easy to offer some form of repair. If you borrow something from a loved one and break it, a meaningful apology would benefit from an offer to replace it. It's not always clear or even possible to do this, but if you can, it helps.

6. Acknowledging that you violated expectations

You can rebuild trust in another person only if you have reason to believe they won't do it again. Making clear that whatever rule or norm you violated is one you ordinarily respect and abide by, and being explicit about exactly what actions you intend to take to stop it from happening again, is important.[3]

On self-forgiveness

Even if the other person has forgiven you and moved on, do you forgive yourself? Many people have a tendency to needlessly suffer for years after everything has long been forgotten by everyone else. We know it's hurting us and holding us back from making any headway with our lives toward something more fulfilling, but we cannot let go. Just saying you forgive yourself does not change how you feel about whatever you did. So where do we begin with self-forgiveness?

One of the biggest obstacles to moving on from a transgression is the common misconception that forgiveness suggests that what happened was justified or not a big deal. We morally want to hold ourselves to account because we think that forgiveness correlates with forgetting or no longer caring about what happened. But on the contrary, forgiveness is a process of taking full accountability and responsibility for our actions. This is not an easy process of carelessly disregarding what happened. It is often painful, especially if what we did caused life-changing harm to another. We struggle to believe that we deserve any such forgiveness, and so we continue to mindlessly self-punish by sabotaging all the endeavors that could make life better for the future.

Self-forgiveness does not happen the moment you decide you want it to. It is a process of making amends for what you have done, putting in real effort to change certain things so that you can feel confident you won't slip up again, and in doing so, having reason to loosen the stranglehold that intense guilt can have on your life. You can get to a place where you are able to accept your fallible nature as a human being and trust that when you make mistakes, you will work hard to repair them and then continue to live the most purposeful and fulfilling life that you can.

Here are a few steps to include in the process:

1. When people write about problems they have been keeping inside, things that seemed overwhelming can be simplified and clarified in the mind so that it becomes more apparent how to resolve and learn from them. Spending time writing things down as you reflect on mistakes is always going to be helpful.[4]

2. Take time to both experience and express in words what you feel. Try to name the various emotions that come up for you. Then consider what it is about your perspective on the event that reinforces such feelings. For example, it might be

unrealistic expectations you hold for yourself, about which you should have known better, or a belief that taking a certain action says something fundamental about who you are and your worthiness.

3. It can be helpful to write out a description of what happened and then to read through and remove any judgment, whichever way that judgment sways. For example, you may notice at points you added in things that sound like qualifiers or excuses. Perhaps more likely, if you are struggling with guilt, is the tendency to add in negative judgments about yourself or to overemphasize the negative impact the actions had. Try to remove all of those and keep your description to just facts.

4. Next, spend time on the various circumstances that made you vulnerable to this mistake. This is very different from a list of excuses; rather, it's an understanding of how you got here. This is in fact an important part of taking responsibility for both the past and the future because if you can understand what led up to your transgression, then you are much better equipped to prevent similar things happening again. It is also a path to the compassion that is necessary in order to move on from self-condemnation. Assuming that you made this mistake because you are inherently bad helps nobody involved and gives you no incentive to do better in the future. Instead, recognize that to be human is to be fallible, but to be human is also to be learning all the way through life. Such a perspective leads to much better outcomes for both you and the people you want to do better for. So don't be

tempted to skip over this part. If your intentions were never to cause harm, say it. If it helps, imagine someone you love unconditionally was in your position and consider how you would enable them to be accountable for their actions without questioning their self-worth.

5. Make explicit what you have learned from this experience. What insights do you now have about how you wish to live your life? How has it informed you about the ways you can avoid such mistakes in the future?

6. Make amends. Depending on the situation, this can be a mix of sincere apologies, compensation of something lost, or restoration of trust. While some of this will be directed toward the other person, certain actions that commit to positive change are also for your own self-forgiveness. When you make a plan and keep to it, you can begin to trust in yourself again. Action is a potent tool for gradually cultivating trust, and therefore relieving the guilt and shame felt about the past. The only way to recover from a past you didn't want is by building a future you do want.

7. Going through this process once is not going to magically erase feelings of guilt. But you have built a structure that you can return to every time the guilt rises up, to remind yourself of the full story beyond mere self-flagellation.

8. Depending on the event itself, the intensity of your struggles with it, and the damage it continues to do to your life, it might be helpful to seek professional support with this process, at least in the beginning.

Takeaways

- The hard truth is that we learn as much about the kind of person we want to be by getting things wrong, as we do from getting them right. Feelings of guilt, regret, and remorse are your signal that there is learning to be done.

- Your regret is not the problem. But your reaction to it might be. Emotions are a best guess about what is going on, so your first position should be to ask yourself if this feeling is warranted. If you have a tendency to constantly second-guess yourself and ruminate on everything that is wrong with the decisions you make, then regret might well be a symptom of that destructive pattern.

- If you genuinely made a misstep and find yourself remorseful about it, then those feelings can be a force for good if you are brave enough to examine them.

- There are some things only adversity can teach you. So let it do so. Be willing to look at the thing you least want to look at, not as a source of self-loathing, but as a source of wisdom.

- Ruminating (thinking over and over) on the things you feel most ashamed of will corrode your own sense of self-worth, and you'll struggle to move on. When we are steeped in shame, we cannot think clearly, let alone learn.

CHAPTER 26

When anger erupts too often

Anger, if not restrained, is frequently more hurtful to us than the injury that provokes it.

—Lucius Annaeus Seneca

A letter from me to you

When you go through a period of losing your temper more often than you'd like, it's easy to slip into deep waves of guilt and shame that make it even harder to get back to your normal self. Nothing brings up sweeping statements about what a terrible person you must be more than losing your temper. The anger steers you in a direction you don't want to go, and it doesn't fit with who you want to be, so the pain that follows is agonizing.

You already know how you would prefer to treat the people you love. But in the heat of the moment, anger is so intoxicating with its sense of power and the promise of a win that it's difficult to let go of.[1] Anger narrows your focus to a purely defensive and protective drive so that sometimes the image of how you want to show up here gets entirely railroaded and you just go with it, saying or doing the things that you know cause deep hurt.

But this is not how it needs to be. Learning how to recenter and refocus in these moments will help you bring your best to the relationships that mean the most to you, even when you feel angry. But when anger is erupting more often than it has in the past, that is worth examining.

The only way that work is possible is through dropping the self-judgment about the fact that this is where you are. Turning anger on yourself is not the same as dealing with it, and being hard on yourself about having expressed anger won't help you keep your cool in the future. If anger is bubbling up in situations that you usually have more tolerance for, then this is an opportunity to learn how to bring your best, even in the hardest situations.

It's easier to do this when you realize that anger is not inherently bad but a normal human emotion like all the others. Its purpose is to gear you up to take a stand and protect yourself when you need to. Unless expressing anger puts you in danger (e.g., in an unsafe relationship), then it does not need to be suppressed. It needs to be listened to, without letting it take over the controls. The reason you can't let anger lead the way is that it nearly always offers you a point of view that is void of the other person's perspective. Once we have that insight, we often feel differently about the situation and choose an alternate course of action.

You could call anger a last-resort emotion. It appears when we lose our sense of being able to deal with the situation in any other way. Sometimes that's because we need a few more skills under our belt for communicating assertively, or maybe it's because there is so much going on in our life that our stress response is already active, so our body is already prepared to act quickly on impulse rather than think carefully through the details. At the end of a stressful day, anger is all that's left. It's the fight in your fight-or-flight. On a better day, our reaction would have been more measured. We would have been able to easily access our own knowledge about how best to deal with the situation.

The good news is that you don't have to brandish yourself as a bad person and live with this forever. There are plenty of ways you can work on understanding this so that you can start bringing your best to your relationships once again.

Real-time tools

Keep in mind that while anger can be informative and tell us when we need to speak up, resolution and the solving of problems comes once anger has calmed and we have the headspace to make careful decisions. Our job when it comes to anger is to know when it threatens to take command of our actions and to do what is needed to remove ourselves from the situation if necessary and bring ourselves back to a state of calm so that we can minimize damage.

This section is front-loaded with the real-time tools first. In moments of anger you can turn straight to this page and remind yourself of how to return to a state of calm and focus that you need in order to deal with things thoughtfully while avoiding harm to others or yourself.

Some of the later tools are more long-term in their approach. Examining what's going on in your life to make you vulnerable to this increase in anger will lay the groundwork for better times, better relationships, and better interactions.

Looking at the moments when we've been at our worst is by no means easy. In fact, it can be horrifying to see the destructive urges that come up and to consider the damage we are capable of in moments of anger and fury. The impulse might be to blame yourself or to relieve the guilt by blaming others. Neither of those options is especially helpful to you when you're trying to work through it. They make change more difficult than it needs to be. As you try to formulate what has made you vulnerable to this, remember that this is not a blame game. It's an examination of your life. The more you understand what makes your anger worse and what makes it better, the quicker you can get back to being you, on a good day.

Bring your body back to calm

Bringing yourself back to an optimal state for dealing with this situation involves taking command of both your physical state and the focus of your attention. Starting with the physical, the most powerful way to de-escalate the physical sensations that come with anger and to calm the body is to breathe in a way that slows everything down.

You have some options here. Some people like to focus on counting as they breathe (breathe in, 1, 2, 3, 4; breathe out, 1, 2, 3, 4, 5). But that is not for everybody. Others like to use one of the many apps available that allow you to breathe in time to a moving image. The general rule is that you want to slow the breathing down to something that mimics the natural rhythm of your breathing. That slow, easy breathing that comes so naturally when you are calm. It is something you can do anywhere, even in the situation that has brought about the anger. Here are some prompts you can follow to do just that.

Try this: You can sit or stand, but pull your shoulders back and open up your posture to allow you to take those slower, deeper lungfuls of air.

- If your jaw is clenched and your shoulders are up high, let them drop to release that tension.
- If you can, breathe in through your nose and out through your mouth. We are not trying to tightly control it, just see if you can allow your breathing to settle into its soothing natural rhythm. Notice how your body will do that for you.
- If you want to slow it further, try counting to three or four in between breaths.
- As you spend a few minutes in that natural rhythm of your breathing once again, you might notice the intensity of the anger come down with it. You begin to gain a little more clarity on the feeling and the situation.
- Even after calming the body, rerunning thoughts of the situation can easily trigger another surge of emotion, so be sure to spend some time on the tool that comes next.

Bring the mind back to calm

There is power in stopping to acknowledge, even internally, that this moment is a real struggle. As you use your breath to bring your body back to calm, allowing the angry voice to continue shouting in your mind about whatever injustice you are up against is like pouring gasoline on a fire you are trying to put out.

Take the reins on that inner self-talk with something that validates the feeling without letting it take control. Here are some examples to get you started.

- This is really tough. It makes sense that I am feeling angry in this situation. I know that letting anger lead is not going to serve me.
- Resolution is rarely found in anger. But plenty of regrets are born there.
- Anger gives me only my own perspective, so I will not be weakened by letting it take control of my next move.
- Once I find calm, I can find a response that will make me proud.
- My best decisions will almost never come in these moments, so let's pause, stop engaging, and wait for the mist to clear and the best strategy to come into view.
- This is my cue to pause and find calm.

Statements like these are much more help to you than anything that sounds like a rant toward you or the other person. They don't tell you what to do, but they turn you in the right direction. Some people find it especially helpful to hold a hand over the chest while saying these words. A compassionate touch that helps to channel your attention and reroute the mind from anger to calm.

You don't have to use these examples. Feel free to write out your own, and then say it to yourself when you most need to refocus. The important part is using the words that resonate most for you so that they turn the dial on your emotional state.

A useful way to frame anger in your mind is that it is the sounding of your internal smoke alarm system that tells you to do something, fast. But, like any smoke alarm, it can only go on the clues available. So it can sound when there is a fire. But it will sound just the same if someone is burning the toast. Your job is to take over and work out what is needed: a calm and measured response or a more dramatic one.

Disengaging for a moment while you let the mist clear does not mean that whenever you feel anger you automatically let the other person off the hook or that you assume their perspective was acceptable. Not at all. When you stop and consider the situation from more sides than your own, you still might come to the conclusion that their position or violation of you is unacceptable. But from here, the intense anger that would not have served you well has a chance to dissipate, and as a result you are much better placed to use the residual anger to your advantage, with a well-thought-out response that keeps in mind your core values about how you want to show up in such instances.

Don't punch a pillow

Despite the widespread belief that anger is some sort of steam that needs to be let out, punching a pillow when you're angry is not helpful if you want that anger to dissipate. This old idea that physically expressing anger in a violent way can be cathartic and vent an emotion that might otherwise stay pent up inside you has been extensively scrutinized in research studies and consistently shown to be not only wrong but potentially harmful.

Hitting a punching bag while thinking of the person you feel angry toward will leave you feeling more angry and vengeful, not less. And aggressive urges increase rather than diminish. If your aim is to feel less angry in everyday scenarios, then widening the narrowed perspective that we have when we're angry is the key.

If we can begin to calm the body and the mind, then our capacity to get a bird's-eye view of the situation as a whole becomes easier.[2]

Formulate what is going on

If you find yourself being angered by things that you normally cope with more easily, then it's time to pause and ask yourself what is going on. Look past those triggers at the wider context of your life.

It's important to remember that these are not justifications, just considerations. Insights that will help you review what happened in a more constructive way. The more you do that, the more patterns you will start to see in your own behavior. That in itself gives you the power to see it coming early enough to choose something different.

As you write down your answers to these questions, you will begin to build a picture that helps to make sense of why this last-resort emotion is coming up more. You can start to get a sense of how continuously ignoring your basic needs and numbing or suppressing stress is like holding air under water. Eventually it will find its way to the surface, usually when you least expect it.

Once you have an idea of the myriad of things contributing to the problem, you can get to work on deciding what changes are both possible and most likely to help. This examination of your life can enable you to do the more preventative work of deciding what needs to change. Some pressures we can't control. Others we have some agency over, even if it's uncomfortable to make choices based on our own well-being. Sometimes the most difficult decisions are the most powerful ones we can make.

"Sometimes the most difficult decisions are the most powerful ones we can make."

Try this:

- Try to answer each of these questions with basic facts before rushing into your own assumptions.
  - List all the things that might be contributing to that lowered threshold for stress.
  - When was the last time you rested?
  - When was the last time you got enough sleep?
  - When was the last time you had a chance to just play at something you love doing?
  - When did you last see your friends?
  - Are you always fighting to keep up with a relentless schedule?
  - Are you eating well?
  - Are you carrying a heavy mental load for work and/or family?
  - When is your chance to refuel and recalibrate?
  - What has been on your mind?
  - What have you been worried about more recently?
- Write down the perspective you held at the time that came with the surge of anger and any assumptions that made the anger seem like the best reaction. Were any assumptions made about malicious intent? Or perhaps expectations about what the other person should have known or considered about you or others?
- Try to spend some time with the possible perspectives of the others involved. How might their intentions have differed from your initial theory? See if you can spend time exploring how their thoughts and motives might be different.

You do not have to believe any of them as fact. Remember, we are simply acknowledging that our first idea about the situation is just one possible perspective. What other intentions would have felt less infuriating or might have even induced a sense of compassion?

- Now shifting from the situation, let's see if you can bring the person into view a little bit more. If you know the person, take a few moments to bring to mind some of their redeeming qualities, things you like or even admire about them. Was there any possibility that the situation reflected their own struggles? Can you engage with a sense of compassion around that? Sometimes it can be helpful to acknowledge times when you have been facing your own struggles and then presented in ways that might have frustrated others without intending to.

As you interrogate the situation and gain this broader, top-down view, write down the insights that you can take forward with you. Formulating constructively in this way can help you feel less victimized by unfortunate circumstances and more in control of your next move.

Understand where it's coming from

Addressing your current needs and circumstances is the best place to start, but if anger has been a long-standing problem, then it can be necessary to consider experiences further back. The brain is always using past experience to help make sense of the present. For example, if you were punished harshly as a child for expressing anger in any form, then you might have learned to suppress it quite well. Then you could spend your adult life numbing or avoiding those feelings, building up resentment and bitterness as you go. But as soon as your guard is down, something that seems small triggers an uncontrollable explosion of rage and a response that appears way out of proportion to what just happened.

This almost instantly reinforces in your mind that anger is unacceptable and dangerous and shameful. So even the experience of it feels threatening, urging you to go around the cycle again by returning to the habit of denying that anger arises, squashing it down, and smiling when you need to be asserting yourself and protecting your boundaries.

If you suspect there is more to this increase in anger than your present circumstances, then working on that demands not a real-time tool but a longer-term piece of work. If you have access to a therapist, they can help you explore the nature of those past experiences and their influence on the cycles that you feel stuck in today.

Doing this work gives the distance we need from anger to bring calm more easily. A big part of therapy also often includes assertiveness training. That work is vital for preventing outbursts of anger that cause damage to relationships because the more tools we have to communicate effectively in a calm state, the less likely anger is to arrive. It gives you the tools you need to have the difficult conversation long before you get angry and the ability to assert your boundaries before they are breached. Talking you through this process would require a whole book in itself, but you can get more details on assertiveness in chapter 5, "When you keep saying yes but you want to say no."

Takeaways

- If it feels like anger is creeping in more and affecting your relationships, this is not how it needs to be. You do not have to be at the mercy of this.

- Turning anger on yourself is not the same as dealing with it, and being hard on yourself for feeling anger won't help you keep your cool in the future.

- Anger is there to keep you safe. But that means it will narrow your focus to a purely defensive and protective drive, railroading your original intentions for how to deal with the situation.

- Anger is the fight in your fight-or-flight. It's the smoke detector whose job is to sound the alarm and direct you to what feels urgent. But it has only so many clues to go by. That's why you must stay firmly in the driver's seat. It is your job to listen to it and work out how dramatic or calm and collected your next actions need to be.

- Arm yourself with the skills to communicate assertively and reduce the need for this last-resort emotion. Also arm yourself with the skills to bring the body and mind back to calm when anger tries to take over.

- Don't punch pillows if your aim is to find calm. It doesn't let off steam, it makes you feel more angry and vengeful.

- Anger will weaken your argument in most situations and damage the relationship further. For that reason, taking control of anger is the opposite of backing down. It is taking time to ensure that you tackle this in the best way possible.

Appendix

Throughout this book I have shared various tools and practical exercises for you to try in difficult moments. Although in the book they all appear in relation to a particular situation, many of the techniques are transferable and you might find them equally useful in other scenarios or to help deal with other challenges. So here I have gathered them together for quick reference, making it simple to refer back and put them to use whenever you need.

Setting boundaries
(From Chapter 5: When you keep saying yes but you want to say no)

When you are so used to saying "I don't mind" as a blanket response for all options presented to you, it's easy to lose a sense of yourself as a person with preferences and to envisage what life might be like if you advocated for them. So take some time to build that insight.

If you don't have a clear idea of what you're aiming for, you are much less likely to get there. So take some time to cultivate a picture of what you're working toward by writing out detailed answers to the questions below.

Let's imagine that you spent a day going about your various tasks and interactions with the firm belief that your own preferences, values, and principles were valid in equal measure to everyone else's. For the whole day you committed to not trampling on your own needs.

- What would that look like?
- In real, concrete terms, what would you do differently?
- Where would the word *no* appear that it hasn't so far?
- Where would you need the most courage?
- What would you stand to lose and what would you stand to gain?
- Now, imagine you did that successfully every day. After one year, how might life look different for you?
- How would the people in your life also benefit?

The no-send letter
(From Chapter 7: When your parents got it wrong)

This is something that is often done in therapy. It is one way to get clarity on relationships that are confusing and layered with conflicting memories and interactions. If you know that your parent will never be capable or willing to listen and talk with the aim of resolving things, or if it seems impossible to speak without interruption or a fight, then this can be an interesting exercise to help work out what you can let go of and how you want the relationship to go forward, even without that person to collaborate with.

Write a letter to the parent in question. Given that you never intend to send this letter, it doesn't matter too much about the order of things or how you say them. Just use this as an expression of all the things you would like to say and would like to ask them. Write down the patterns of harmful behavior, the effects of them, and how you intend to break those patterns going forward.

Write down how you feel about this parent and the relationship you are going to take responsibility for having with them from now on. The letter can include an offloading of all the most hurtful things they did, the special moments they ruined, the betrayals or abandonments, the cruel words. But also take time to explore the things they did for you that you feel grateful for, to recognize how they might have exceeded the standards of their own upbringing.

Remember, this letter is never to be sent. It is for you and your own clarity of mind so that you can act with informed and carefully thought-out intention.

Self-compassion technique
(From Chapter 8: When you get it wrong as a parent)

Place your palm over your chest and hold it there for a moment.
Allow your breathing to slow back to its natural rhythm.
And feel the warmth of your hand radiate on your chest.
Allow everything to slow.
Then say these words to yourself, either out loud or in the quiet of your own mind:

- This is tough.
- I am trying my best with what I have right now.

- It feels so painful when I get it wrong because I care so deeply.
- It is love that enables me to steer back in the direction I want to go after I fall.

Allow yourself to sit, breathe slowly, and repeat any of these words that might have resonated for you, or find your own, until you feel able to return to the challenge you're facing. These moments of recentering can be small: a deep breath and a few words to yourself in the most challenging of scenarios that shifts the focus of your attention and clarifies in your mind how you intend to approach this. Alternatively, recentering can be used as a part of longer meditations that can aid in accessing a form of self-compassion. For those who would like to use longer guided meditations, these can be found for free on my YouTube channel (@DrJulie).

Accessing self-compassion
(From Chapter 12: When it's hard to ask for help)

It is very easy for someone on the outside to see you as worthy of help, but much harder to get that objectivity in our own view of ourselves. One way to do that is to spend a few moments answering the following questions.

Take all the problems you are facing right now and imagine that it's not you who is facing them at all. Imagine the person in your life you would least want to have these problems. What would it feel like to know they were facing all this?

If this person you care about deeply was facing this, what help would you want to give? Knowing what you know about the situation, what help would you see as most pivotal?

But now, imagine that you cannot help them in this way because, well, you don't know what they are dealing with. They decided to struggle alone and not ask for help. They know that asking for help could lead to better days ahead, but they see all the same barriers that you see.

Notice how the idea of that scenario feels substantially more painful, knowing how eager you would be to help, if only they would let you in.

Notice how you judge the situation, whether you think any less of the person for the context they find themselves in, or whether you simply see another human being who could do with a helping hand.

Picture that loved one and ask yourself: Do you see them as worthy of help?

Knowing the situation well, what help would most benefit them?

What would you want them to have the strength to do?

If you could, how would you reassure them that the best thing would be to ask for help?

And, if you see that person as worthy of your help, then you owe yourself the chance to be helped in the same way.

Planning to ask for help
(From Chapter 12: When it's hard to ask for help)

Anything that feels initially overwhelming is easier to tackle when we break it down into concrete steps. Make a conscious effort not to look too far ahead, just get clear on the task in front of you.

Write down a list of the people you could approach for help, with the most approachable at the top.

Next, write down exactly what you need: a listening ear, distraction, practical support, or simply connection and friendship. Once you have that clear in your own mind, it's easier to be concrete in what you are asking for. You won't have to think on your feet too much and risk slipping into more avoidant strategies like dropping hints. People are just as poor at responding to hints as they are to full-blown mind reading, so clarity is your friend.

Visualization tool for finding confidence

(From Chapter 14: When you doubt yourself and want to feel more confident)

For this quick experiment, it might be helpful to write down your answers so you can refer to them afterward.

Take a few moments to imagine that, by some miracle, you woke up and your confidence in yourself had magically blossomed. From the moment you opened your eyes in the morning, how would you know this had happened? When you answer this, try to focus less on how you might *feel* differently and more on exactly what you would *do* differently and how you would do it. How would you hold yourself? How would you move? How might you interact with people differently? How would you approach upcoming challenges? Try to consider the finest details of difference. Paint that picture in your mind and use it to construct a list of actions.

Most people, when they dream in this way, assume that they must wait for that feeling or problem to change before the story can come true. But much like the problem of motivation, confidence is not a feeling that comes first. So everything on the list you have created, those are the actions that will in fact help to invite that feeling. Some things on the list will feel more possible than others. Why not start with those?

Confidence is the bus that never arrives while you sit waiting. It usually makes an appearance after you have decided to walk and you're almost at your destination. So get to work on making some progress, and I'll bet the bus arrives once you're a little ways down the road.

Grounding exercise
(From Chapter 15: When you feel overwhelmed)

If you are feeling stuck in a state of immobility or tension, this short exercise gives you a break from overwhelming stimuli and a chance to reconnect with your body in the here and now and reorient to the present moment.

Put your feet on the ground as you begin.

Notice what else you can touch nearby. Whether it's your clothes, the wall, or the chair you're sitting on, just take a few moments to explore that thing, as if for the first time.

Observe and then describe in your mind how it feels: the temperature, the texture, the weight of it in your hands.

Now look around and find something in this space that you haven't paid much attention to recently. Maybe because it's not that interesting, just something you tend to pass by without much thought. Spend a few moments getting more familiar with that object, observing and describing in your mind once again. You might notice how the light falls on it, the colors and shadows, textures and lines. What words would you use to describe this thing?

Now expand that awareness to pick up on the sounds you can hear. Some of them might come from nearby, others might seem far away. You're not trying to judge or change any of those; simply notice, observe, and then describe them in your mind.

You can keep doing this, looking for things in your immediate environment that you can touch, see, and hear. This is the process of using your senses to bring you back into the present moment when your mind may have taken you off to thoughts that trigger stress and overwhelm.

You can also combine this tool with self-soothing, a great technique for tolerating high levels of distress when you need to get through tough moments. This also involves using each of your senses. But this time you choose to focus on things that you associate with safety and comfort. For example, here in England the ritual of making and sharing tea is heavily associated with closeness and comfort that when we slow that process down and take notice of each step—paying attention to what we see, hear, and smell as we pour and brew our cup—it can help relieve overwhelm and emotional distress. These soothing sensations can be found in anything, including the perfume of a loved one, a traditional family meal, photographs of happy times, music that calms. You get to choose the details. The key is that you are using each of your senses to bring you into the here and now and soothe your way through distress rather than trying to numb it or escape it.

Figuring out what matters most
(From Chapter 17: When you're scared of making the wrong choice)

It is much harder to make decisions when we are being pulled in different directions that seem to contradict each other. So it makes sense to work out how much weight to give to each of those influences. Our values and priorities change as we go through life, and a brief check-in with those is always a good idea when there is a big decision to be made. There are different ways to do this, which I cover in more detail in my first book (see chapter 33 of *Why Has Nobody Told Me This Before?*). But when you are focused on a specific decision, this is an easy way to make sure that your choice is based on what matters most to you at this point in your life.

Write down a list of the different aspects of your life that are likely to be affected by the decision you face. Examples include family, parenting, friendships, intimate relationships, career, health, education, personal development, community, and contribution.

Next to each of these different areas, write down a few words in answer to the following questions:

- What is most important to you about this area of your life?
- How do you most want to show up and contribute here?
- How will the choice that you face affect your capacity to live in line with these values? Will it bring you more in line with them or further away?
- How will you feel about that? Will that enhance your life or diminish it?

Depending on the gravity of the situation you are facing and the different values that it conflicts with, you can spend as little or as much time with this as necessary. The only requirement is that you are willing to be truly honest with yourself in the process. Not as easy as it sounds. Often, the answers we get are not the ones we want to hear. Especially if we realize that the choice we need to make is the most difficult one.

Technique for taking the leap
(From Chapter 17: When you're scared of making the wrong choice)

When we are contemplating making a change, but so far have been unable to commit to it, we might weigh up the advantages and disadvantages of change. We can see clearly if benefits outweigh the costs. But then we can't understand why we still feel hesitant to start. This simplistic analysis has missed something crucial.

Something that we all seem to overlook is the payoffs of doing nothing. The ways in which *not* taking action on this choice rewards you and allows you to avoid something. Once you have identified those payoffs, you can get honest with yourself about what inaction is costing you and will continue to do so over a lifetime.

This is an insightful exercise when you already know the choice you need to make but have been avoiding taking action on it. You can use the following questions as prompts.

- What are the payoffs in holding back on this decision?
- What does it allow you to avoid?
- What does that cost you now and in the future?
- Are you willing to live with the consequences of that?

Finding willpower for change
(From Chapter 18: When you're short on willpower)

One mistake most people make when trying to find the willpower to act is to pay heed to the trends promoted online that involve visualizing how wonderful everything could be once you reach the end point of a goal, imagining you are already there, and reminding yourself of all the reasons you want to achieve it. While there is some merit in that, here is a less gentle but somewhat potent tool for activating yourself.

First, it's helpful to also get real about two things:

1. The payoffs you experience for not starting today, that serve to keep you stuck. This means acknowledging that you hold on to a situation you no longer want, not just

because it's hard to make the change, but because there's a strong pull to keep things the same. In choosing something new, you may also have to let go of something.

2. The true consequences for you in keeping things the same. Inherent in this is the acknowledgment that not yet choosing to change is still very much a choice. This enables you to fully engage with the consequences of today's actions, rather than perceiving it as merely a delayed choice.

Spending a few minutes writing down your answers to these questions can help you gain clarity on the push and pull we can often feel between the prospect of change and keeping things the same.

- In holding back, what are you protecting yourself from? What are the downsides of this change that you are avoiding?
- What benefits or comforts do you enjoy now that you would have to let go of when you take action?
- What gains are you missing out on when you don't take action?
- What is it costing you personally every time you choose to keep things the same?
- If you don't see this through or you fail to even begin, what will that mean for you?
- How will that affect your estimation of yourself?
- How will it affect the things in your life that matter most to you?

Anticipate challenges ahead
(From Chapter 18: When you're short on willpower)

When we are trying to make positive change and we face temptation from the options we need to avoid, and a reluctance to take action that we know will benefit our future, we can learn a lot from the most extreme cases of this work: addictions. For those in treatment for addictions, a significant amount of time is spent on relapse prevention. This means planning for the worst days, anticipating all the potential hurdles, and creating a detailed, concrete plan to tackle each one. Without doing this early on, you leave your future in the hands of your impulses.

When something is difficult enough to require willpower, this work will undoubtedly be a worthwhile investment of your time. List all possible threats to your success. This is the time to use self-doubt to your advantage. Allow those worst-case scenario thoughts to run riot for a few moments, knowing that this is part of a more constructive process than simply ruminating on them. We are about to round them up and cage them in with a strong and well-thought-out plan to prevent each one from sabotaging your goals.

Building a plan to minimize chances of failure can require some difficult decisions on your part. It might involve saying no to things that you previously enjoyed or valued, and saying yes to new change that fills you with fear and uncertainty. Rather than allowing this to deter you from the effort ahead, keep the reasons for this goal front and center in your mind. Maintain absolute clarity on why you want this and why you *don't* want the alternative.

Appendix

- What are the barriers and obstacles ahead that pose a risk to your success?
- What are the times, places, or situations that, if left to impulse, would create a roadblock to your progress?
- What are all the excuses and justifications you might use to make it feel more acceptable to slip off track in those moments?

Once you have a list of all the potential barriers, set about creating a plan of action for how you intend to navigate each one.

While this is an uncomfortable process, what's more anxiety provoking is not knowing what is coming. Running into hurdles full force because you didn't see them coming diminishes your chances of seeing your goal through. But being brave enough to look ahead at the things that are going to bring challenges, and the way you would approach them that would bring about failure, means that when the time comes, you just have to follow the plan for navigating them without too much disruption to your forward momentum.

Connect with your future self
(From Chapter 18: When you're short on willpower)

Absorbed in all the demands of day-to-day life, most of us never take the time to think too far into the future. It all feels far away and less relevant than everything on our plate right now.

Studies have shown that when we feel disconnected from our future self in this way, we are more likely to disregard the future consequences of today's actions. We tend to be more impulsive and make choices based on how we want to feel now, not what we want for our future.

If we don't want to mistreat our future selves and give them more to deal with through today's impulsive decisions, it helps to get in touch with the realization that the image of you in the future, is not an idealized version of you with no challenges. In fact, effort will feel, in the deepest sense, very much the same as it feels today.

Take a few moments to close your eyes and imagine yourself a week or a month from now, looking back on the choices you are making today.

How does your future self feel about those actions? How will they have affected your future?

Now see if you can write a note to that future self and tell them what you are going to do now to make life better for them. What do you need to take action on today to make sure that you in the future looks back with pride and gratitude and a new sense of momentum toward better things?

Bring your body back to calm
(From Chapter 26: When anger erupts too often)

Bringing yourself back to an optimal state for dealing with this situation involves taking command of both your physical state and the focus of your attention. Starting with the physical, the most powerful way to de-escalate the physical sensations that come with anger and to calm the body is to breathe in a way that slows everything down.

You have some options here. Some people like to focus on

counting as they breathe (breathe in, 1, 2, 3, 4; breathe out, 1, 2, 3, 4, 5). But that is not for everybody. Others like to use one of the many apps available that allow you to breathe in time to a moving image. The general rule is that you want to slow the breathing down to something that mimics the natural rhythm of your breathing. That slow, easy breathing that comes so naturally when you are calm. It is something you can do anywhere, even in the situation that has brought about the anger. Here are some prompts you can follow to do just that.

- You can sit or stand, but pull your shoulders back and open up your posture to allow you to take those slower, deeper lungfuls of air.
- If your jaw is clenched and your shoulders are up high, let them drop to release that tension.
- If you can, breathe in through your nose and out through your mouth. We are not trying to tightly control it, just see if you can allow your breathing to settle into its soothing natural rhythm. Notice how your body will do that for you.
- If you want to slow it further, try counting to three or four in between breaths.
- As you spend a few minutes in that natural rhythm of your breathing once again, you might notice the intensity of the anger come down with it. You begin to gain a little more clarity on the feeling and the situation.
- Even after calming the body, rerunning thoughts of the situation can easily trigger another surge of emotion, so be sure to spend some time on the tool that comes next.

Understand your anger or stress

(From Chapter 26: When anger erupts too often)

If you find yourself being angered by things that you normally cope with more easily, then it's time to pause and ask yourself what is going on. Look past those triggers at the wider context of your life.

It's important to remember that these are not justifications, just considerations. Insights that will help you review what happened in a more constructive way. The more you do that, the more patterns you will start to see in your own behavior. That in itself gives you the power to see it coming early enough to choose something different.

As you write down your answers to these questions, you will begin to build a picture that helps to make sense of why this last-resort emotion is coming up more. You can start to get a sense of how continuously ignoring your basic needs and numbing or suppressing the stress is like holding air under water. Eventually it will find its way to the surface, usually when you least expect it.

Once we have an idea of the myriad of things contributing to the problem, you can get to work on deciding what changes are both possible and most likely to help. This examination of your life can enable you to do the more preventative work of deciding what needs to change. Some pressures we can't control. Others we have some agency over, even if it's uncomfortable to make choices based on our own well-being. Sometimes the most difficult decisions are the most powerful ones we can make.

- Try to answer each of these questions with basic facts before rushing into your own assumptions about it.

Appendix

- List all the things that might be contributing to that lowered threshold for stress.
  - When was the last time you rested?
  - When was the last time you got enough sleep?
  - When was the last time you had a chance to just play at something you love doing?
  - When did you last see your friends?
  - Are you always fighting to keep up with a relentless schedule?
  - Are you eating well?
  - Are you carrying a heavy mental load for work and/or family?
  - When is your chance to refuel and recalibrate?
  - What has been on your mind?
  - What have you been worried about more recently?
- Write down the perspective you held at the time that came with the surge of anger and any assumptions that made the anger seem like the best reaction. Were any assumptions made about malicious intent? Or perhaps expectations about what the other person should have known or considered about you or others?
- Try to spend some time with the possible perspectives of the others involved. How might their intentions have differed from your initial theory? See if you can spend time exploring how their thoughts and motives might be different. You do not have to believe any of them as fact. Remember, we are simply acknowledging that our first idea about the situation is just one possible perspective. What other intentions would have felt less infuriating or might have even induced a sense of compassion?

- Now shifting from the situation, let's see if you can bring the person into view a little bit more. If you know the person, take a few moments to bring to mind some of their redeeming qualities, things you like or even admire about them. Was there any possibility that the situation reflected their own struggles? Can you engage with a sense of compassion around that? Sometimes it can be helpful to acknowledge times when you have been facing your own struggles and then presented in ways that might have frustrated others without intending to.

As you interrogate the situation and gain this broader, top-down view, write down the insights that you can take forward with you. Formulating constructively in this way can help you feel less victimized by unfortunate circumstances and more in control of your next move.

Acknowledgments

Thank you to Sienna, Luke, and Leon for being my anchor point and constantly reminding me what matters most. Thank you for putting up with me when I have been tired or absent while writing this. I promise to support you in discovering and achieving your dreams, the way you have done for me.

Matthew, I have more to thank you for than space to type. Somehow, we have found ourselves on this wild and beautiful journey, and there is no one I would rather go with. Thank you for taking on such a heavy load of responsibility so that I could focus on this book. I don't know how you do it. Thank you for your patience in giving me the time even when you were bursting with new content ideas. Thank you for always being a source of energy for me, amplifying my drive, injecting fun into everything, and finding gratitude even at times when you have lots to complain about. And thank you for putting such a great title to the idea for this book.

A very special thanks to Lucy for welcoming me to YMU with open arms. It has been a dream to work with the best in the business, and your ideas and opinions will always hold such weight for me. Thank you, Ellie, for never missing a beat, knowing exactly where I should be, what I should be doing and when, and for supporting me through event after event. I am especially grateful to you both for keeping the world at bay so that I could write. Thank you to Guy for being brave enough to join our team and for taking it all in stride. Thank you especially for magically making all the work disappear when I found myself facing hard times.

Thank you to my agent Amanda Harris for all your endless supply of help and encouragement along the way, from the proposal on scrappy paper to a shiny book on the shelf. You have been there to help whenever I need it.

Thank you to my editor, Ione Walder, for patiently waiting in the wings while I tried to create something that was good enough to show you, always supporting and encouraging. Thank you for helping me turn this into a book we want to shout about. I am so grateful to get to work with you.

And thank you to Daniel Bunyard for your kind support all the way along and for constantly inspiring me with the breadth and depth of your knowledge of all things books. I still have so much to learn from you.

Thank you to Louise Moore for seeing the potential in my proposal and for making this book possible. A special thanks to Ciara Berry. You are always such a pleasure to work with, and your hard work helped us get my first book out to more people than I could ever have imagined. Let's get ready for round two.

Thank you to all the Penguin Michael Joseph family. It is truly a privilege to work with you all, and I am so proud to have that MJ symbol on my books.

Thank you to Judith Curr at HarperOne in the USA for seeing the potential in this book.

Thank you to Rachel Mills and your exceptional team, Alexandra and Charlotte. You truly are a dream team.

To Mum and Dad, I owe you everything. Thank you for your constant support throughout this journey. The work ethic you instilled in me seems to have paid off, and you continue to make that possible by being there for the children whenever I need to work. And Mum, you shared with me the story of your friend's daughter that eventually led to the idea for this book.

Thank you to my sisters, Claire and Sarah. You both have taught me more than you know. Thank you for understanding my absence and encouraging me to reach high. And thank you for being there when times were tough.

Thank you to Pat and David. You are a constant source of inspiration and support, and Matthew and I are grateful for you both every day. None of this would have happened without Matthew, so I hope we have both done you proud.

Thank you, Jackie, for always understanding and never judging me for the mess after a busy week. Without you I would be a quivering wreck surrounded in chaos.

Thank you to Ben Garner for all your hard work behind the scenes and your consistent enthusiasm even when I have been locked down writing and unable to produce new content.

Thank you, Sean, for always being there to hold the fort and support Matthew in everything. We are deeply grateful and lucky to have you.

Thank you to everyone who read my first book and then shared it with friends and family or left generous reviews. I am forever grateful to each and every one of you for such unwavering support. Without it, I may not have been brave enough to write another one. I hope this book will earn its place on your bookshelf and make itself useful as you forge ahead in your life.

To the army of clinicians and researchers I have learned from over the years, your work has been crucial in the creation of this book. Please accept my apologies for any errors or omissions in how I have made sense of it.

Thank you to my clients for trusting me with some of your most painful and vulnerable experiences. I often wonder how each of you are getting on. This book is about the words we might need to hear, but you have each taught me when to stop searching for the right words and simply let the silence fill the space between us.

For anyone who would like more on these subjects, my You-Tube channel and Instagram @DrJulie contain videos based on the ideas from this book.

Notes

Chapter 1. When you compare yourself and come up short

1. Michael Pemberton and Constantine Sedikides, "When Do Individuals Help Close Others Improve? The Role of Information Diagnosticity," *Journal of Personality and Social Psychology* 81, no. 2 (2001): 234–46.

2. Alain de Botton, *Status Anxiety* (London: Penguin Books, 2005).

3. Leon Festinger, "A Theory of Social Comparison Processes," *Human Relations* 7, no. 2 (1954): 117–40.

4. Herbert W. Marsh and John W. Parker, "Determinants of Student Self-Concept: Is It Better to Be a Relatively Large Fish in a Small Pond Even If You Don't Learn to Swim as Well?," *Journal of Personality and Social Psychology* 47 (1984): 213–31.

5. James A. Shepperd and Kevin M. Taylor, "Ascribing Advantages to Social Comparison Targets," *Basic and Applied Social Psychology* 21, no. 2 (1999): 103–17.

6. Oliver James, *Affluenza: A Contagious Middle Class Virus Causing Depression, Anxiety, Addiction and Ennui* (London: Vermilion, 2007).

Chapter 2. When your friends are not your friends

1. Robert Greene, *The Concise 48 Laws of Power* (London: Profile Books, 2002).

2. Eric Berne, *Games People Play: The Psychology of Human Relationships* (London: Penguin Life, 2016); Stephen B. Karpman, *A Game Free Life: The Definitive Book on the Drama Triangle and Compassion Triangle by the Originator and Author* (San Francisco: Drama Triangle Publications, 2014).

Chapter 3. When you want to be less awkward around people

Dale Carnegie, *How to Win Friends and Influence People* (New York: Simon & Schuster, 1936), 101.

1. Geoffrey L. Cohen, *Belonging: The Science of Creating Connection and Bridging Divides* (London: W. W. Norton, 2022).

2. Philip G. Zimbardo, Paul A. Pilkonis, and Robert M. Norwood, "Social Disease Called Shyness," *Psychology Today* 8, no. 12 (1975): 69; Bernardo Carducci, "Shyness: The New Solution," *Psychology Today*, January 1, 2000, Psychologytoday.com.

3. David Brooks, *How to Know a Person: The Art of Seeing Others Deeply and Being Deeply Seen* (London: Penguin Books, 2023).

4. Lynne Henderson, *Improving Social Confidence and Reducing Shyness: Using Compassion Focused Therapy* (London: Constable, 2010).

Chapter 4. When you feel unwelcome and want to fit in

1. Geoffrey L. Cohen, *Belonging: The Science of Creating Connection and Bridging Divides* (London: W. W. Norton, 2022); Iain McGilchrist, *The Master and His Emissary: The Divided Brain and the Making of the Western World* (New Haven, CT: Yale Univ. Press, 2009).

2. David Brooks, *How to Know a Person* (London: Penguin Random House, 2023).

Chapter 5. When you keep saying yes but you want to say no

1. Lisa Feldman Barrett, *Seven and a Half Lessons About the Brain* (London: Picador, 2020).

2. Marsha M. Linehan, *Skills Training Manual for Treating Borderline Personality Disorder* (London: Guilford Press, 1993).

Chapter 6. When you're dealing with passive-aggressive people

1. Edward McIlduff and David Coghlan, "Understanding and Contending with Passive-Aggressive Behaviour in Teams and

Organizations," *Journal of Managerial Psychology* 15, no. 7 (2000): 716–36.

2. Ramani Durvasula, *It's Not You; How to Identify and Heal from Narcissistic People* (London: Vermilion, 2024).

3. Scott Wetzler, *Living with the Passive-Aggressive Man: Coping with Hidden Aggression from the Bedroom to the Boardroom* (New York: Simon & Schuster, 1992).

Chapter 7. When your parents got it wrong

1. Jasmin Lee Cori, *The Emotionally Absent Mother: How to Recognize and Heal the Invisible Effects of Childhood Emotional Neglect* (New York: The Experiment, 2017); Jonice Webb, *Running on Empty: Overcome Your Childhood Emotional Neglect* (New York: Morgan James, 2014).

2. Ramani Durvasula, *It's Not You: How to Identify and Heal from Narcissistic People* (London: Vermilion, 2024).

3. Eric Berne, *Games People Play* (New York: Ballantine Books, 1966); Stephen B. Karpman, *A Game Free Life: The Definitive Book on the Drama Triangle and Compassion Triangle by the Originator and Author* (San Francisco: Drama Triangle Publications, 2014).

4. Daniel J. Siegel and Mary Hartzell, *Parenting from the Inside Out: How a Deeper Self-Understanding Can Help You Raise Children Who Thrive* (New York: TarcherPerigee, 2004).

Chapter 8. When you get it wrong as a parent

1. Daniel J. Siegel and Mary Hartzell, *Parenting from the Inside Out: How a Deeper Self-Understanding Can Help You Raise Children Who Thrive* (New York: TarcherPerigee, 2004).

2. Becky Kennedy, *Good Inside: A Guide to Becoming the Parent You Want to Be* (London: Thorsons, 2022).

3. For more on the research behind self-compassion, see Chris Irons and Elaine Beaumont, *The Compassionate Mind Workbook: A Step-by-Step Guide to Compassion Focused Therapy* (London: Robinson, 2017).

4. Kennedy, *Good Inside*.

Chapter 9. When they don't love you back

1. Guy Winch, *Emotional First Aid: Healing Rejection, Guilt, Failure, and Other Everyday Hurts* (New York: Plume Books, 2014).

2. Esther Perel, *The State of Affairs: Rethinking Infidelity* (London: Yellow Kite, 2017).

Chapter 10. When they love you but you won't let them get close

1. Jasmine Lee Cori, *The Emotionally Absent Mother: How to Recognize and Heal the Invisible Effects of Childhood Emotional Neglect* (New York: The Experiment, 2017).

2. Jonice Webb, *Running on Empty: Overcome Your Childhood Emotional Neglect* (New York: Morgan James Publishing, 2014).

3. Omri Gillath, Emre Selcuk, and Phillip R. Shaver, "Moving Toward a Secure Attachment Style: Can Repeated Security Priming Help?" *Social and Personality Psychology Compass* 2, no. 4 (2008): 1651–66.

4. Chiara Ruini and Cristina Mortara, "Writing Technique Across Psychotherapies—from Traditional Expressive Writing to New Positive Psychology Interventions: A Narrative Review," *Journal of Contemporary Psychotherapy* 52 (2022): 23–34.

5. James Pennebaker and Joshua Smyth, *Opening Up by Writing It Down: How Expressive Writing Improves Health and Eases Emotional Pain* (New York: Guilford Press, 2016).

6. Linda Hill, *Avoidant Attachment Recovery: Break Free from Avoidant Habits to Build Secure and Long Term Relationships* (Printed in Great Britain by Amazon, 2023).

7. Amir Levine and Rachel Heller, *Attached: How the Science of Adult Attachment Can Help You Find—and Keep—Love* (London: Rodale, 2011).

Chapter 11. When you want to win the argument

Robert Greene, *The Concise 48 Laws of Power* (London: Profile Books, 2002).

1. Julie Schwartz Gottman and John Gottman, *Fight Right: How Successful Couples Turn Conflict into Connection* (London: Penguin Life, 2024).

2. A. G. Grimmer, "The Nine-Part Model: A Tool for Sharing Dyadic Formulations," Bristol CBT, accessed October 17, 2024, www .bristolcbt.co.uk/publications/the-nine-part-model-dyadic -formulation.

Chapter 12. When it's hard to ask for help

1. Jonice Webb, *Running on Empty: Overcome Your Childhood Emotional Neglect* (New York: Morgan James Publishing, 2014).

2. Phil Stutz, *Lessons for Living: What Only Adversity Can Teach You* (London: Vermilion, 2023).

3. John Bowlby, *A Secure Base: Parent-Child Attachment and Healthy Human Development* (London: Routledge, 2005).

Chapter 13. When your inner voice is your own worst critic

1. Paul Gilbert, *Overcoming Depression: A Self-Help Guide Using Cognitive Behavioural Techniques* (London: Constable & Robinson, 2009).

2. Julie Schwartz Gottman and John Gottman, *Fight Right: How Successful Couples Turn Conflict into Connection* (London: Penguin Life, 2024).

3. Lynne Henderson, *Improving Social Confidence and Reducing Shyness Using Compassion Focused Therapy* (London: Constable & Robinson, 2010).

4. Timo Brockmeyer, Johannes Zimmerman, Dominika Kulessa, et al., "Me, Myself, and I: Self-Referent Word Use as an Indicator of Self-Focused Attention in Relation to Depression and Anxiety," *Frontiers in Psychology* 6 (2015), https://www .frontiersin.org/journals/psychology/articles/10.3389/ fpsyg.2015.01564/full.

Notes

Chapter 14. When you doubt yourself and want to feel more confident

1. Russ Harris, *The Confidence Gap: From Fear to Freedom* (London: Robinson, 2011).

Chapter 15. When you feel overwhelmed

1. Jon Kabat-Zinn, *The Healing Power of Mindfulness: A New Way of Being* (London: Hachette, 2018).

Chapter 16. When you hate who you've become

1. Kristin Neff, *Fierce Self-Compassion: How Women Can Use Self-Compassion to Stand Up, Claim Their Power, and Speak the Truth* (London: Penguin Life, 2022).

2. Roz Shafran, Sarah Egan, et al., *Overcoming Perfectionism: A Self-Help Guide Using Scientifically Supported Cognitive Behavioural Techniques* (London: Robinson, 2010).

3. Paul Gilbert, *Overcoming Depression: A Self-Help Guide Using Cognitive Behavioural Techniques* (London: Robinson, 2009).

4. Chris Irons and Elaine Beaumont, *The Compassionate Mind Workbook: Your Step-by-Step Guide to Developing Your Compassionate Self* (London: Robinson, 2017).

5. Mark Williams, John Teasdale, et al., *The Mindful Way Through Depression: Freeing Yourself from Chronic Unhappiness* (London: Guilford Press, 2007).

Chapter 17. When you're scared of making the wrong choice

1. Christopher Hitchens, interview with Andrew Anthony, *Guardian*, November 14, 2010.

Chapter 18. When you're short on willpower

1. Gertraud Stadler, Gabriele Oettingen, and Peter M. Gollwitzer, "Physical Activity in Women: Effects of a Self-Regulation Intervention," *American Journal of Preventive Medicine* 36, no. 1 (2009): 29–34.

2. Steven Pressfield, *The War of Art: Break Through the Blocks and Win Your Inner Creative Battles* (New York: Black Irish Entertainment, 2002).

3. Kelly McGonigal, *The Willpower Instinct: How Self-Control Works, Why It Matters, and What You Can Do to Get More of It* (New York: Penguin Group, 2013).

4. McGonigal, *The Willpower Instinct.*

5. Hal Ersner-Hershfield, Daniel G. Goldstein, William F. Sharpe, Jesse Fox, Leo Yeykelvis, Laura L. Carstensen, and Jeremy N. Bailenson, "Increasing Saving Behavior Through Age-Progressed Renderings of the Future Self," *Journal of Marketing Research* 48 (2011): 23–37.

Chapter 19. When you must perform under pressure

1. Carolyn N. Orson and Reed W. Larson, "Helping Teens Overcome Anxiety Episodes in Project Work: The Power of Reframing," *Journal of Adolescent Research* 36, no. 2 (2020): 127–53.

2. Dave Alred, *The Pressure Principle: Handle Stress, Harness Energy, and Perform When It Counts* (London: Penguin Life, 2016).

3. Marc A. Russo, Danielle M. Santarelli, and Dean O'Rourke, "The Physiological Effects of Slow Breathing in the Healthy Human," *Breathe* 13, no. 4 (2017): 298–309.

Chapter 20. When you're overthinking everything

1. Lisa Feldman Barrett, *How Emotions Are Made: The Secret Life of the Brain* (London: Macmillan, 2017).

2. Russ Harris, *The Confidence Gap: From Fear to Freedom* (London: Robinson, 2011).

3. Kevin Meares and Mark Freeston, *Overcoming Worry: A Self-Help Guide Using Cognitive Behavioural Techniques* (London: Little Brown, 2021).

Chapter 21. When fear shows up

1. Carl Jung, *Letters: Volume 2, 1951–1961* (London: Routledge, 1976).

2. Carolyn N. Orson and Reed W. Larson, "Helping Teens Overcome Anxiety Episodes in Project Work: The Power of Reframing," *Journal of Adolescent Research* 36, no. 2 (2021): 127–53.

3. Lisa Feldman Barrett, *Seven and a Half Lessons About the Brain* (London: Picador, 2020), 79.

Chapter 22. When grief overwhelms you

Colin Murray Parkes and Holly G. Prigerson, *Bereavement: Studies of Grief in Adult Life*, 4th ed. (London: Penguin, 2010).

1. Julia Samuel, *Grief Works: Stories of Life, Death and Surviving* (London: Penguin Life, 2018).

2. Kelly McGonigal, *The Joy of Movement: How Exercise Helps Us Find Happiness, Hope, Connection, and Courage* (New York: Avery, 2019).

Chapter 23. When everything feels pointless

1. Ian D. Boreham and Nicola S. Schutte, "The Relationship Between Purpose in Life and Depression and Anxiety: A Meta-analysis," *Journal of Clinical Psychology* 79, no. 12 (2023): 2736–67.

2. Gary M. Cooney, Kerry Dawn, Carolyn A. Greig, et al., "Exercise for Depression," *Cochrane Database of Systematic Reviews* 9, Art No. CD004366.

Chapter 24. When you feel like an imposter

John Steinbeck, *Working Days: The Journals of "The Grapes of Wrath"* (New York: Penguin Books, 1989).

1. Thomas Gilovich, Victoria H. Medvec, and Kenneth Savitsky, "The Spotlight Effect in Social Judgement: An Egocentric Bias in Estimates of the Salience of One's Own Actions and Appearance," *Journal of Personality and Social Psychology* 78, no. 2 (2000): 211–22.

2. Jean M. Twenge and W. Keith Campbell, *The Narcissism Epidemic: Living in the Age of Entitlement* (New York: Free Press, 2009).

3. Jean M. Twenge, "The Evidence for Generation Me and Against Generation We," *Emerging Adulthood* 1, no. 1 (2013): 11–16.

Chapter 25. When you have done something you regret

Aldous Huxley, *Brave New World*, 11th ed. (London: Vintage, 2010).

1. Phil Stutz, *Lessons for Living: What Only Adversity Can Teach You* (London: Vermilion, 2023).

2. Guy Winch, *Emotional First Aid: Healing Rejection, Guilt, Failure, and Other Everyday Hurts* (New York: Plume, 2013).

3. Winch, *Emotional First Aid.*

4. James W. Pennebaker and Joshua M. Smyth, *Opening Up by Writing It Down: How Expressive Writing Improves Health and Erases Emotional Pain* (New York: Guilford Press, 2016).

Chapter 26: When anger erupts too often

1. Russell Kolts, *The Compassionate Mind Approach to Managing Anger Using Compassion Focused Therapy* (London: Robinson, 2012).

2. Brad J. Bushman, "Does Venting Anger Feed or Extinguish the Flame? Catharsis, Rumination, Distraction, Anger and Aggressive Responding," *Personality and Social Psychology Bulletin* 28 (2002): 724–31.

Find out more

For anyone who would like to learn more about the subjects in this book, my YouTube channel, Instagram, and other social media pages contain videos based on many of the ideas and themes covered here.

@DrJulie

@drjulie

@drjulie

@DrJulieSmith